SPREAD WIDE

KATHY ACKER & PAUL BUCK
REBECCA STEPHENS   JOHN CUSSANS

ENCOUNTERS

SPREAD WIDE

AN ENCOUNTER BETWEEN KATHY ACKER & PAUL BUCK
WITH FURTHER INTERVENTIONS FROM REBECCA STEPHENS & JOHN CUSSANS

Dear Glenda & Paul I am
one crummy letter
writer & here I am back in USA
& hot on new book so don't know
when I'll get back to Urope but
swore to M. Lebel I'd return to
teach class 1/30 so if though no
$ per usual back by then - maybe -
I don't know - I am definitely
bad at life O.K. at writing maybe
this new work (work?) too
wierd - in love with Flaubert -
money from my grand-
mother's will doesn't
come through till August
- so until then am broke as
usual - but I don't give a
shit (except you 2 have gone
to such trouble about house) life as usual
bunch of crummy boyfriends
who don't let go but don't love
me madly casual sex is boring
& all-pervasive I think casual
means masochism I love Flaubert
ain't Christmas wonderful I
intend to eat a hard-boiled egg
for Christmas dinner dedicated

to Bataille -
how's new issue of CURTAINS
going? I wish it was Christmas
all year round so there'd be lots
of dopey Christmas cards to
help (thwart?) my inability to
articulate I
hope Santa
sends me
a nice
boyfriend
but
this
is 1980 so there
are only eggs eggheads

doesn't mean anything new poetry theory

A grandson
fine as you are
Brings a lot of joy
and pride,
And that's how come
this Christmas wish
Has so much love inside!
Merry Christmas!
XXOOXX

Mr. Descartes ruined France
& S&M came out of the
body-mind split oh mechanisms
I bought myself a Roussel
book for Christmas excuse
this drivel it's just to say
a poem! in my inarticulate way
I think love you 2
Kathy -

For You, GRANDSON

In the beginning is the egg. Hard-boiled. Hard-ridden. Whips and cream in the cellar where frustration dies. Where only Wittgenstein is found with any certainty, *complete certainty, a certainty that is all his own*, reading the stories of Norbert Davis. Good stuff, he said, conveying the right tone of voice, *as it were*, feeling completely justified. Wanting to write the pulpster and tell him just that. He who was too whimsical for *Black Mask*. Are you hurt? No, I'm just dead inside. Long past a rendezvous with fear.

At least we'll not get fat on that diet, whipped creams, stuffing for any Xmas display, not trussed but lying on the bed, believe me, spread wide, just another day to relinquish my desires for the betterment of mankind. Better that is meant to find mankind. Any man, any kind, just who will love me. Will want an honest extension of his power. I think. Therefore. I wonder if you will join me for dinner.

Troppmann, the butcher of eight, driven by a book, Sue's *Wandering Jew* shapes his life and his fall, seeing the blade as it accelerates sharply. That one book that had been devoured and used as a bible, a grimoire, scriptures to instruct him in a life of crime, a way of life, a determining factor. That one book that Troppmann had remarked upon: "He who reads many novels, and has them in his head, falls asleep. But he who only reads one, has a fixed idea." And loses his head over it, eventually.

Troppmann, that man who novelizes himself back into a creature of fiction, surfaces with Bataille, like a tale of two cities, and more, first showing his drunken head in London, before reverting to Paris, not at all the narrative of his own crisis but more the reflection of it.

Or does it matter if we chase across the fields of Pantin, out of breath, to unearth whether Lazare represents Simone Weil, or Dirty, not Colette

IS THE EGG MORE THAN THE CHICKEN, OR THE CHICKEN THE IMPORTANCE FOR WHICH THE EGG EXISTS?

H

O

W

TO

E

A

R

N

ENOUGH,

A

N

D

STILL

K

E

E

P

MY CLOTHES ON?

Peignot, or even Xénie? Is the I what this eye sees or just an I on the page? Is the I what the eye sees or the I or not? Is Kathy the K or the Kathy? Or not. Are we more interested in the letters and diaries than the castle and trial? You have to picture the space, the emptiness, the drop that is presented between the name on the page and the real person, to fall backwards out the window like Xénie threatens. That drop into the void, those moments of terror before it happens, as much as when it would be happening.

Is it worth the work involved to cut through the nasal accent, to stress what I desire? I would like to be there. To see you all. To find a cosy home to settle in. Dreams. That's all I ever ask for. But have no money to set it in action, always waiting, will, willing it to come across. Filthy lucre. Smackers. Or some such dish, dosh, ackers, tosh, that is us, like a recipient of an award from a government agency that wants me, you, us, skewered on the table. Hard heads. Like the hard surface of the table rather than the bed. Skewered on the table. Spread wide for their delight. Cock sucking and cunt licking bureaucrats who will never nourish either of us.

Eggstentialism. Eggistence. Egged on to give head, but prefer to refer to my sources. Like that Masson drawing, hanging in the Bataille, the Sadean reference, a good enough reason for a trip to Europe. Oh can I come and live with you folks?

Is the egg more than the chicken, or the chicken the importance for which the egg exists?

How to earn enough, and still keep my clothes on?

Or losing their heads, over little ol' me. But they don't mean it. Better to lose your head on the guillotine. The great drop. Head to the bran. Think it hilarious they translate "son" as "sound" as you told me. Do they all do that? I checked out that addenda to *Story of the Eye* and you are right in the version I have. What a sing song. Where was the Concert Mayol? I really must start learning more before I set sail for the motherland. If the motherfuckers here ever let me leave.

The Concert Mayol only closed in 1979, in the rue de l'Echiquier, just short of Bastille Day, discovered on a backstage photo of girls in the final show, "Erotic aux Nues".

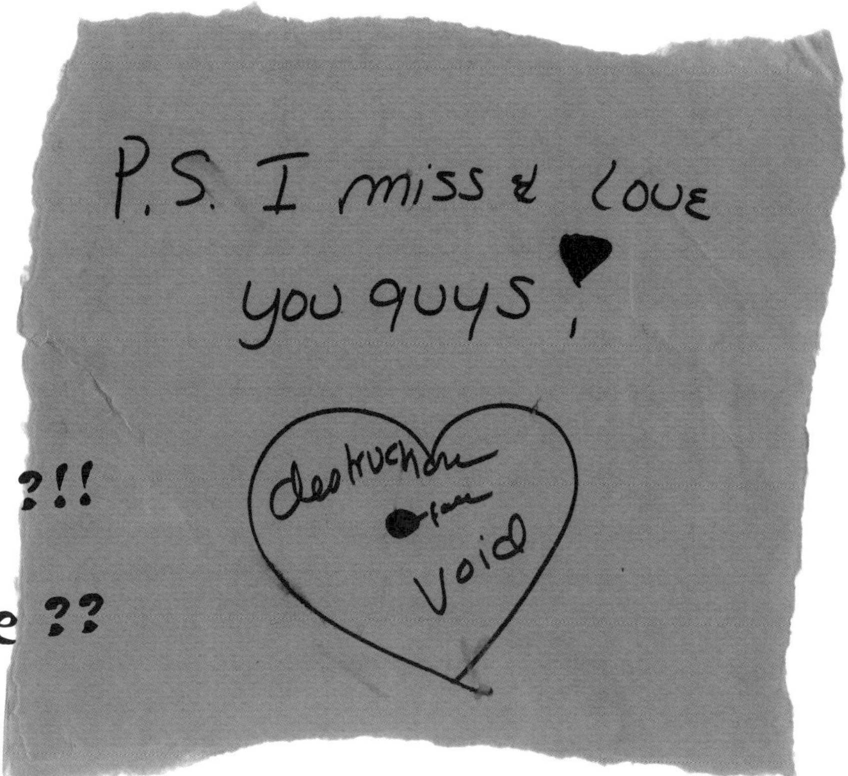

fall ?!!

face ??

fate ?

My name is Paul. That's a suitable name from an Italian mother. Though of course I'm not really Paul, I'm Francis. After he of Assisi, it was stressed. But who wants to be called Frank? So I'm Paul. The disciple of Christ. That's "marked" me for life, as they say. I lived in a neighbourhood where there were no boys. Only girls. My sisters and her friends. Other girls in the street. I used to look up to the older girls, often from below the hems of their skirts. They had creamy thighs. One in particular. I remember the first time I had sex with L, or let's call her Liv, or not, let's call her Mary, in the hollow in the meadow, baring her thighs, barely having time for preliminaries. Did we do preliminaries? Foreplay. Did we know about such things? Nobody was watching. Innocence was blown out the window. That drop through the void, a freefall panic, like the first sperm that creamed my pants, a punishment for not getting the answer correct, for not being able to answer the questions. And yet I was always so good at Biology.

I adored the way thighs fell open, like a book with smooth pages. Though I wasn't too keen to watch others plundering my books, the books I selected. But I couldn't do a thing about it, crawling in the bushes peering through windows to watch neighbours fucking on their living-room floors. Or at least one couple. I was never caught. I was learning, and as with all learning, you had to know when to stop. I never stopped, that was the point. I would turn their key in the back door, the key we kept for emergencies, and slip up the stairs, rummage beneath the bed to find the smutty magazines, or look in the drawers to find knickers. White thighs. As my sighs increased. Until one day I was of size enough to take the step myself, to jump in at the deep end.

Neighbours were always moving. New ones meant new experiences, though always back to square one. No, perhaps not. I learnt from each experience. I had my tricks.

So what happens when one knocks out one's partner in the spasms of love? Charging around the room, falling over, locked together, tumbling, clambering up, but trying to remain joined, tripping, unbalancing, so unnatural to keep one's balance in this state, and then the inevitable, falling, not just hurting oneself, one has been doing that all along, bruises, minor

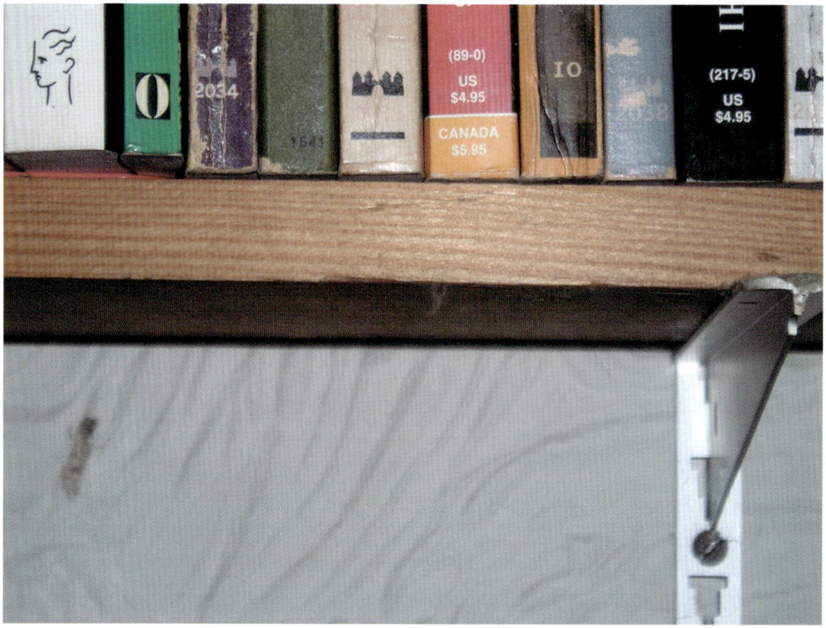
O
2034
(89-0)
US
$4.95
CANADA
$5.95
IO
(217-5)
US
$4.95

abrasions, mindful not to damage one's sex, but not paying enough attention to our heads, not until, clomp, her head hits a surface, a wall, the edge of a table, anything will do. Not just a minor knock, but a knock, a complete accident, I told the officer, no not that far. But enough to knock her unconscious. That sudden panic to see if she was alive. She was. No panic. Subsidence. She was breathing. The need to fetch a damp cloth, to carry her to the bathroom, to splash cold water on her face. Or just to sit there for a moment, to regain one's own senses and ponder her position, like a doll, that one can move around, spread the legs, bend the legs, move the arms, play with, funny gestures, lewd gestures, do whatever one wanted. Kiss all over. But one does that anyway, what is the fascination to do that when the other is unaware, is unable to participate? Is this the start of a pleasure for necrophilia? To do what then?

There is nothing quite like passion when one hasn't seen one's partner for some while. A week. A month. Sometimes even a weekend. Less. That sudden desire, shared by both, to rip clothes off and throttle each other into oblivion, to fuck each other stupid. What senseless craving drives us to these heights? Or depths? To find myself trapped between thighs nestling the soft flesh in my mouth. Moments of bliss. Mouthfuls.

When I was a young I used to roam the woods, the air raid shelters, the ruins of the old mansion, burnt out, that belonged to Lord Waring. I list these places, all had the same fascination for me, a fascination that had been determined in the bunkers. Feeling my way in the semi-darkness, I had walked into a web, one that plastered itself across my face, a web, a mask, that stuck to me, paralyzed me, momentarily, and which I soon realized was living. Tingling. Something I soon realized was a spider. Instantaneously I was terrified, that horror everyone has of the spider, that unreasonable horror as if it will claw, bite or savage us in some way. It was there, not threatening. It had lost its web, a web that was worn across my face. It too was trapped for the moment, then it was gone, scurried away.

One learns. One realizes webs are everywhere in these dark explorations of the abandoned. I started to look for them, to study their inhabitants, those queens of their castles, waiting for their prey. I was never

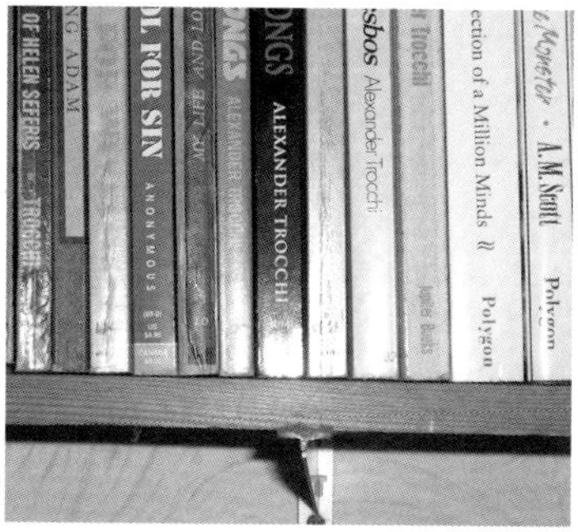
OF HELEN SEFERIS
TROCCHI
NG ADAM
OL FOR SIN
ANONYMOUS
ALEXANDER TROCCHI
sbos Alexander Trocchi
ection of a Million Minds
Polygon
A. M. Scott
Polygon

their prey, but I could have been their potential destroyer. Yet I felt no desire to destroy. I developed a desire to stand before them, as one stands before the altar, looking in fascination at those sacred traps that became objects of worship. Desires grew to stroke them, those queens, to caress them.

No wonder when I discovered women, my fascination lay between their thighs, the lure that fascinated me, drew me. That I became devoted to, devouring it as it devoured me.

He is inventing a way of not writing even as he writes, wrote Duras, regarding Bataille. He teaches us to unlearn our literature.

RESOURCES

Ludwig Wittgenstein: Ray Monk

On Certainty: Ludwig Wittgenstein

Rendezvous with Fear: Norbert Davis (aka the Mouse in the Mountain, aka Dead Little Rich Girl)

Murder for Profit: William Bolitho

Blue of Noon: Georges Bataille (trans Harry Mathews)

The Blue of the Sky: Georges Bataille (trans Paul Auster & Lydia Davis)

Oeuvres Complètes III: Georges Bataille

Georges Bataille: Michel Surya

Ecrits de Laure: Laure (Colette Peignot)

Eroticism: Georges Bataille

The Little One: Louis Trente (Georges Bataille) (trans Paul Buck)

Story of the Eye: Lord Auch (Georges Bataille) (trans Joachim Neugroschel)

The Childlike Life of the Black Tarantula: The Black Tarantula (Kathy Acker)

White Thighs: Frances Lengel (Alexander Trocchi)

Outside: Marguerite Duras

WHILE I AM STANDING MY FEET GO STRAIGHT INTO AIR AND I REMAIN STANDING

Dear Paul and Glenda,

How wonderful to hear from you. Excuse suck such (now you know I'm sick!) sich prompt reply on my part, but work's getting heavy these days so if I don't reply fairly quick I get all entangled... Just got phone call from James Sherry asking Do you know Paul and Glenda? Let's have dinner and talk about them. So will, tomorrow night. Ridiculous flu for two weeks now, ever since I went to Mudd Club three o'clock A.M. New Year's Eve with bottle of cheap champagne in me (like baby) guy whom I know only as friend of friend kisses me. I keep my lips closed cause I'm not attracted to him and I know he's gay he bashes me to floor I'm too fdrunk to know if on purpose or not the corner of my head next to eye smashes agaainst sharp protrusion bang bang the bouncers, the next thing I know, I pulling this guy off me. I stumble back to my feet. Dazed I say to bouncers Don't kick him out he's friend of mine. They don't. I figure I'm hurt but too dazed to figure out anything else. Head of Mudd Club Steve says Let's go to back room do coke. I usually don't do coke and do now twenty lines, Steve keeps shoving it up my nostril I guess cause he wants to seduce me then fills me up with bottle of Dom Perignon. At this point I am total zombie while I am standing my feet go straight into air and I remain standing. People look at me and say OH. But I can't express what I want, WHICH IS MY BED, cause I'm zombie and I can't figure out how to get this (me) to bed. Then Steve says Let's eat breakfast and I go cause I can't speak. We go to place of cats' piss it is the most disgusting place I've ever been to even though this guy from running Mudd Club's a millionaire. Then he drives to his apartment with out

Been sitting on this roof for some days now, wondering what the fuck I'm doing here. I mean, **New York New Year, starring Kathy Acker**. Instead of a sexophone we have Rhys cracking guitars. Or just some of the guys that Peter's involved with. Shit, they'll all be famous one day. Just like me, who is NOTHING. How many times do I have to say it? But nothing is what it's all about. Meaning is the last straw.

I mean: Do I have to sleep with you?
I MEAN: DO I *HAVE* TO SLEEP WITH YOU?
How many others ways do they want me to say it?

Rhys crashes a chord, and I come in his face.

Well, my dear, let's cut to the chase. I'm actually going to make it, I'm going to get there much sooner than you think. Than I think. There I go again, thinking. But the more I think about it the more anxious I am to do it. So get the food ready. I'm joking of course. I don't do food. Just coke. Or lines of prose. I just can't stand being here much longer. I get terribly weak, worse than that, cos of overwork. But that's how it's always been, nothing new about that, I want to work, I plunge in and devour myself in the process, and then I feel weak and threaten myself never to do that again. I should just invite boys round, fuck them, get them to pay me, that would be a better way to conduct my life. It's a way to stray from my path. I would want to come at once. Get me a garret, I don't need a house. I need to starve to achieve it. I need to tap into all those people sitting in the cafés, to live their lives, to get inside them, to make me more than a nobody.

Here everyone wants to draw me into their quarrels. I need to avoid all quarrels. It ain't healthy. I can't draw from them, their lives are zilch.

They want me to follow their course, to trace the same lines as them. Fuck them. I know what I want, WHAT I NEED. I want to turn to them and say FUCK YOU. But I'm a good little girl, I refrain. I try not to sing it again. See how they let me enter their rhythms and patterns. Again and again. Same old refrain.

So it's better to be up here, to try to clear my head after the binge of everything that has entered my body... drink, drugs, germs... and all those words: *demonstres ubi sint tuae tenebrae*. Oh yeah, thin bra. Oh yeah. Or tiny bra, tiny tits. Skinny old me.

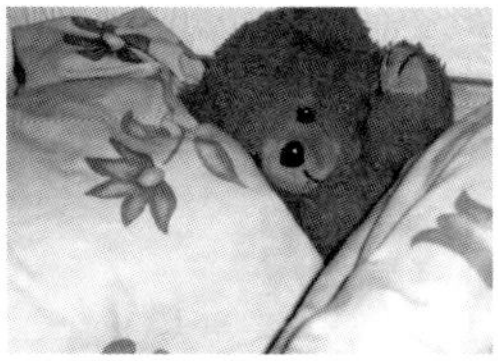

asking me if I am interested which I think is very bad manners almsot as bad as cats' piss. But he rents out his upper floor to Viva who's away for holidays so even in my zombieness I can make attempt to see if there anything from a certain M. Schull (Schuhl?) whom I had great night with before leaving Paris and whom Viva recently wanted to marry but he, according to her, turned out to be too selfish, according to me is just great lush sex. Of course I find nothing and can speak nothing Mr. Steve keeps asking me how he can seduce me. I am sitting on his bed with my coat still on cause I am too zombie to take it off and besides this Mr. Steve is NOt attractive, it is just I am too zombie to have figured out until this moment that he wanted to sleep with me. Most of the time it is amazing when a guy wants to sleep with me cause I am you know just me I am nobody. So I say Do I have to sleep with you? which is the first sentence I've been able to manage. He says I'm not a cad. I say O.K. and get up to leave cause I want my bed most of all I want my stuffed animals. Mr. Steve chases me and yells at me downstairs I walk home and it is now 10:00 A.M. New Year's.

HAPPY NEW YEAR

I sleep two hours and then everyone calls to ask if I'm going to this party and I realize I have awful hangover so awful I don't realize until about 6:00 I've been beaten up pretty severely my whole face is swiollen my friend Bets says One quarter inch higher, kid, you would have died. So immediately after, but probbably due

Here I am inclined to fight solipsism, because I cannot yet say the thing I really want to say.

DO I HAVE TO SLEEP WITH *YOU*????

Oh how many more times do you want it, to kiss or to fuck, it's all the same if you kiss me a thousand times, then a hundred, then a thousand again, then a hundred, and then a thousand, then a hundred, and once aroused confused, dazed and confused, we'll know no sum that an eye may envy while the count goes on, another thousand, then a hundred… until we're all fucked out.

da mi basia mille, deinde centum,
dein mille altera, dein secunda
centum , deinde usque
altera mille, deinde centum. dein,
cum milia multa fecerimus,
conturbabimus illa, ne sciamus,
aut nequis malus invidere possit,
cum tantum sciat esse basiorum

So, I ask again: How many more times do I have to sleep with you? Or do you just want to beat up on me?

There are times I feel like a cripple, a hideous cripple, emotionally as much as physically. Cos all I want to do is fuck. Fuck. Fuck. Fuck. What am I going to do with my life? How am I ever going to make any money? Just cos I come from a family with money, it don't mean I have money.

FUCK FUCK

Roof. To be in the gutter, and to love the gutter. To make money in the gutter, that's rock and roll.

Just when I think I've started writing, that the story is going somewhere, that the narrative is going somewhere, I have a total seizure. I fail. On a grand scale. I have to start again.

LA DI DA

Is it that you really want of me that I tell thee the truth – as I see it? Make sense he said. But I don't want to make sense. Why does it all boil down to making sense? Stop making sense.

LA DI DA

To spread my legs doesn't mean I'll be loved, just fucked. May as well go to the brothel. TRA LA LA

The only thing that can get close to the brothel is the library. Stick it next door. Or opposite. Get in there with the books. He might think books will change the world, oh hell no, he thinks his cock is going to change the world. TOTALLY. You wanna know the difference between him and those others I

to germ warfare, of course not to beating up I get this lousy flu, which I've had now for two weeks, it's like heavy having (bad typing creates puns) mumps or V.D. in the wrong place, no sex, so stupid, so I read Husserl. Any object of consciousness is real. How's that for simplification? No, I'm not worried about money, I'm too sex-fiend even if I am a little celibate these days cause of getting burned badly over holidays by... but we won't become morbid ...one boy 2 boys 3 4 5 6 7 8 ...hee hee...but I have to do all these lousy performances cause I'm broke and I'm a lousy performer so can't get back to Europe till June when have money after California tour, alos two new books out, one in March, BLOOD AND GUTS in spring FINALLY well, I think children should SLAVE for their parents (who else is going to?) Want to loan me a child? I need affection these days. All sex, no affection. Solipsism wind. Not power, solipsism. At least power presupposes human connections. The states of the world are boring. Back to Catullus. I'm not being clear, am I? I'm not clear. I'm sick of meaning. Enclose beginning of new work on subject.

I love you guys. Am reading Daumal now (in between Hussyroll). And Dickens. DICKENSFDICKENSDICKENSDICKENSDICKENS. Don't want to be a liberal now. I love you two. Of course please do a "feast" I'll send the beast in a few days, but want to get this letter to you now because it is so TRASHY I hate PUNK ROCK, in answer to your question, I HATE FASHION I NEVER MAKE JUDGEMENTS I GIVE UP MUOST OF ALL I GIVE UP. And I don't know how to type.

Love
Acker

pick up in the street, those nobodies? Well, I can speak to them. You try speaking to writers you fuck.

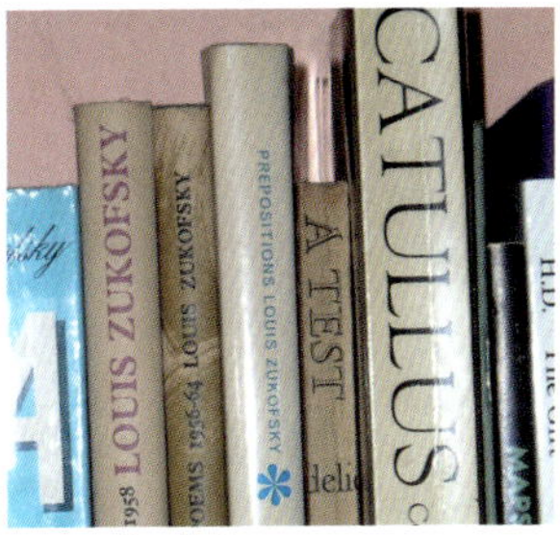

It's a bit like Cluedo, 'cept it should be fucking, not murder, even if fucking can be murder. In the library with the ten inch. With whom? Theo or Paul. Pat Garrett. Come again? Doubt it. Get real. Get serious.

I like to be pounded every day, bruised, naked flesh against naked flesh against naked flesh until I ache and ache and ache. I always ache. I need love. Affection.

I hit him in the name of liberty. I hit him in the library. Do you fuck for money, or for free? When society refuses you the right to existence, you must take it.

I like to think and I don't trust people who think.

Patience my little ones. I will persevere. I always persevere.

One of those shits who tells me what I must do, how I must write, showed me his work, and that of his friends. And it's all bloody alike. Well I'm different. Absolutely different. I want the truth, my truth, my story. I don't want the deadness they write.

I want my truth, but do I want to model everything on myself, do I know myself, do I want to model on my friends, and I do have friends, I should just take from who and what and where and how and who and what and where I like and just say I, I, I say I, and I mean I – do you remember that crazy & LOVELY film by Zulawski called *Possession*? Piercing reality. Because you say I for me, says Adjani. (CHECK IT OUT). I I I. I say I, and I mean YOU YOU YOU, ALL OF YOU.

So I get to Paris. Or London. So I get out of here. How much we have to expend to achieve. One never gets back what one puts into something. Yeah, but then art is not about money, unless you are starving. Do I starve? Of food, sometimes. Of love, always. Of sex. Haha.

As Vince said, I'm losing the desire for marriage and children. Am I sad? I guess I am. You think that one day you'll start wanting all that. But in fact, I'm retreating, refraining, that again, from that line of thought, of action. Or as I saw somewhere, someplace, a book somewhere, someplace: THE LOVE OF ART MEANS THE LOSS OF TRUE LOVE.

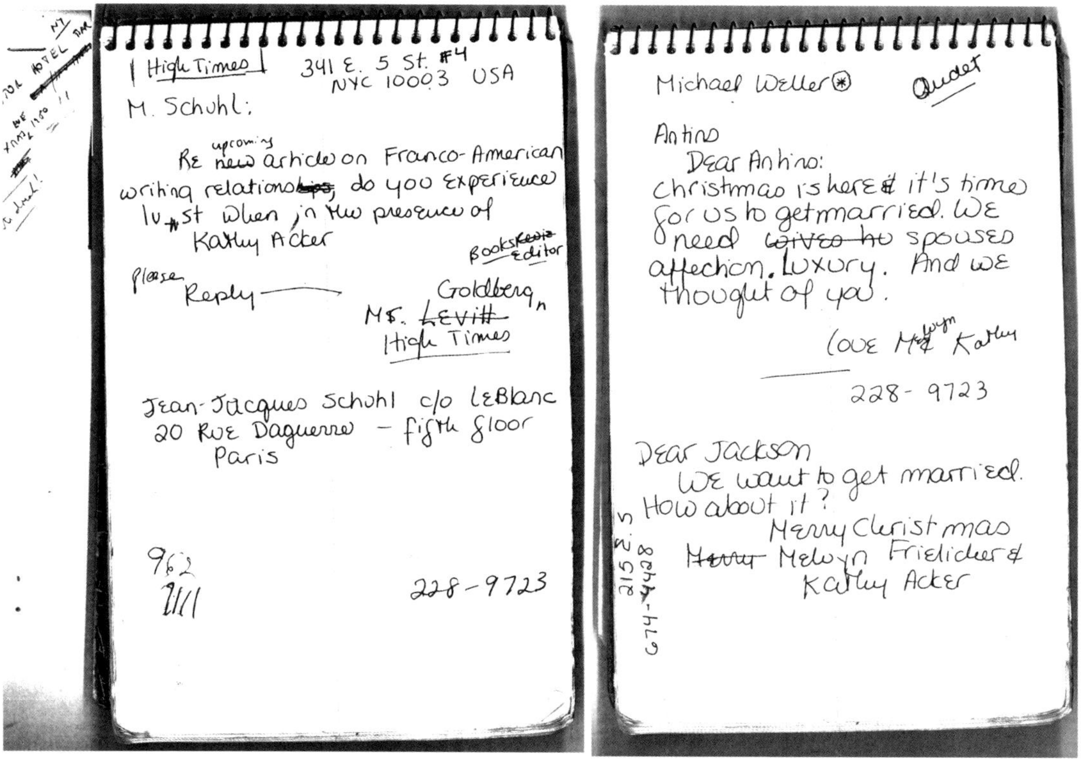

Written in Astor Hotel bar, New York, Xmas Eve 1980 — *Melvyn Freilicher*

So fucking true, or what? – but on the other hand true love makes you disgusted with art. Did I say that? **Did I say that?**

So I feel old and tired at times, sometimes. But my spirit isn't broken. To succeed one has to have ambition, be ambitious, and you know what I think about ambition, it sucks. I'm going to become a burden on everyone. I'm going to live right under your skin, and you'll not be able to say a thing about it. Or write a word. They'll all know nothing about it.

The 'noise' title as far as I'm concerned is a joke. And to call my music noise is to completely miss the point. If you think of that huge chord that you heard in the performance yesterday; one way of taking it would be to hear it as a wall of sound. Another way would be to see it as carrying 6 or 7 different melodies, all taking place at the same time. What is actually going on is incredibly complex musically. If you take the lower E string of the guitar, there are a number of overtones that are generated by that string – 13 in all. If you're in the key of E, the fundamental overtones would be E, an octave above that, B, perfect 5th, octave, major 3rd, perfect 5th, minor 7th, 8th overtone, B octave, major 2nd in relation to that. And they get closer and closer together and by flatpicking directly with the string, you can get those overtones and make melodies within the framework of one note. So what we've done is to train our ears to hear these overtones very well. Now this is just working with one string. There are 6 strings on a guitar, so as soon as you start adding them, the musical picture becomes increasingly complex. It gets denser and denser until, when you have all 6 strings on all the guitars, with all the overtones shimmering around, there are so many voices going on that the tonality becomes atonality and starts to sound like one voice.

I could write pieces, texts, like *Guitar Trio*, or *Drastic Classicism*. Rhys showed me how to extend my arms. I like this idea that I can be Rhys one day, Robert Longo the next, a gunslinging guitarist if ever I saw one. And then shit, me again, Kathy. What a din. Perhaps I could get together a hundred writers and get them to write a paragraph each, I can make a list. I just did. I realize that I personally know 100 writers at this time, so I don't think it would be a problem to get them to write my book. I can email them. They will have to be tutored, I reckon 5 rehearsals will be necessary. I can divide them into six groups, give them different pens to write with, or different fonts. It makes such a difference when you write with Palatino or Verdana, let alone any of

DEAR JOHN___

MERRY CHRISTMAS! & AS THE NEW YORK
TIMES'S MOST NEEDY CASES:
PLEASE ENGAGE KATHY A + MELVYN F
IN SOME FORM OF MENAGE TROIS BOTH
TO INSURE AFFECTION, MONEY + LOOSE SHOES.

L.W.

[LAWRENCE WEINER]

the fancy stuff like Apple Chancery, or come to that Times New Roman as opposed to Times.

It makes such a difference when you write with **Palatino** or Verdana, let alone any of the fancy stuff like Apple Chancery, or come to that Times New Roman as opposed to Times.

It makes such a difference when you write with Palatino or **Verdana**, let alone any of the fancy stuff like Apple Chancery, or come to that Times New Roman as opposed to Times.

*It makes such a difference when you write with Palatino or Verdana, let alone any of the fancy stuff like **Apple Chancery**, or come to that Times New Roman as opposed to Times.*

It makes such a difference when you write with Palatino or Verdana, let alone any of the fancy stuff like Apple Chancery, or come to that Times New Roman as opposed to **Times**.

No, I can't do that. That's what comes from hanging out the clubs. To be in at the birth of the cool of each generation, Mudd in New York, or UFO in London. What in Paris? They never had music in Paris. Not real rock & roll, not first hand, anyhow.

So what story do you want to hear now? A bedtime story?

My name is Jacqueline Onassis. No, that's not right. My name is Kathy Acker. No, wrong. My name is Steve. No. Well, we were in this club. Or out of it. Out of our heads. In his bed. On his bed. He thought he could get it up me like the black stud who coked me and blew my head off, leaving me wanting more, quivering for more, leaving me in mid sentence, a death sentence.

Now think on this while you await another blast. In a city like Paris everyone everyday everywhere in the place has the possibility of being killed. Work out the odds yourself. Of course you can avoid these odds, if you decide not to go out at all, but to stay at home, get the rest of your family doing the same. To do that would be nuts. Day in day out. You'd die. Starve to death. To be wise, or not to be dumb, you go out each day, you face the possibility of death, you risk your life. Accidents will happen. They got to happen to someone. Terrorist action will happen. Someone has got to be blown up. So you take some precautions, fill your pockets with things you might need. Most importantly, you look right and left when you cross the street, just like you were taught in primary school. You try not to walk under ladders when men are working at the top of them, carelessly. You avoid the dark corners of life. You look up, you look down. But you do no more than that. You don't consider every action as a potential death trap the moment before you take it, unless you really do want to drive yourself into a death vortex.

Kathy's real name is Charles Dickens, not Georgy Eliot. Just she don't know it yet. But she's been thinking about it, her expectations are high. She met Charles on the film set of A TALE OF TWO CITIES, he was trading under the name of Dirk Bogarde. More glamorous that way. Of course that way there's only one outcome. Someone is going to lose their head over someone else. & you know who that person is going to be?

So Kathy is walking around as the headless one, acephalous, tottering, playing with fire, headless, yet happy within her head, wanting Lacan to run with the ball, the experience being the way, ultimately. So A TALE OF TWO CITIES is going to become ROMEO AND JULIET. But Kathy don't know that yet. She don't know that she will star as Colette Peignot, and that Bataille will fall for her and she'll be slobbering at the leash, the giving of oneself entirely to limitless abandonment.

How much coke does it take to realize how fucking great Noé's *Irreversible* is? You would, wouldn't you? What? Pulp a guy like that, knock his fucking brains out, unremittingly, if your woman had been fucked to death. All fired up, all coked up.

The idea of standing, with one's feet going right up in the air. Still standing.

All she wants is love. Don't you understand? Compris? Love, all she wants is love. A Janis crying her eyes out in a haze on her bed.

I'm not really strong on bass. I don't really know too much about it. But Michael, the bass guitarist, does. He has a special technique of playing the bass where he hammers the strings directly on the fretboard. What we do is work on a time framework, which we call units. Michael has made this 64 beat phrase. It's totally unbelievable. But at first I was a little worried about the bass line, because it was a melodic thing and I didn't want a melody to be defined because the music should be able to tell a story without telling a story. In that sense, there might be a relationship in the music to the 'new image' artists.

To write a book, to create any art, where the temperature is made so that nobody feels comfortable. Some shiver and others sweat. That's how it should be.

When we read this word "I" without knowing who wrote it, it is perhaps not meaningless, but is at least estranged from its normal meaning.

Husserl: Logical Investigations

By this time I was no longer capable of speech, even of interior speech; my mind travelled too rapidly to carry any words along with it. I realized, in a sudden illumination, that I still had control of the hand which held the pencil, that I still accurately perceived the position of my body, and that I could hear and understand words uttered nearby – but that objects, words, and meanings of words had lost any significance whatsoever. It was a little like having repeated a word over and over until it shrivels and dies in your mouth: you still know what the word 'love' means, for instance, you could use it correctly, but it no longer truly evokes its object. Or indeed its subject.

I need to start again. To get to grips with a narrative. What about:

She slipped out of the bath and into her lipstick. Five minutes later she was dead.

Or fifteen. Let's give it the Warhol touch. Fifteen minutes later Viva was dead. Just gives us time to write the book. To narrate fifteen minutes of her life.

RESOURCES

Catallus (trans Celia & Louis Zukofsky)
The Adult Life of Toulouse Lautrec: Henri Toulouse Lautrec (Kathy Acker)
The Letters of Vincent Van Gogh
Possession: Andrzej Zulawski
Towards a Musical Agenda for the Nineties: Rhys Chatham
Rhys Chatham interview 1981
Meditations: David Antin
A night of serious drinking: René Daumal (trans David Coward & E.A.Lovatt)
A Fundamental Experience: René Daumal (trans Roger Shattuck)
Georges Bataille, la mort à l'oeuvre: Michel Surya
La Communauté Inavouable: Maurice Blanchot

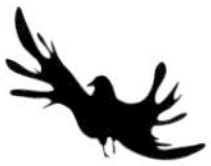

Dear Glenda and Paul, I'm just about to run off to my friends Peter and David's house (around the corner) to play CLUE which is my favorite game in the world besides chess, but I can't find anyone to play chess with me; playing CLUE is like reading ten Agatha Christie stories all in a row and then there are always more (THEN THERE WERE NONE) so real life is better than fiction. So I shall tell you a story FROM REAL LIFE.... (and not tell you about the marvellous secret CLUE society we are forming)...

James Sherry...

That pig disguised in lamb's clothing, now I don't mean to make judgements, I never have opinions no not me he....

Mr. Sherry who I only know most casually as a poet, a business connection you might say, and a very failing business, calls me up one day and says, "Oh, you know Glenda and Paul. Let's have dinner one night and discuss them." Well, my dears, don't get your nasty little egos about, we didn't discuss you at all, we discussed I don't know what something about how my books are all fantasy WHICH THEY ARE NOT THEY ARE TRUER THAN LIFE so I knew he was stupid but being a woman and womanly kept my fat trap shut . And then he says I write satire and he wants to go beyond satire, and I replied that I was much too stupid to write satire; to write satire one had to be capable of making judgments and then only thing I'm capable of is rebellion i.e. I just put down what I hear. Then he says that my main problem is I don't cut up enough I still have stories. I tried to explain that my friends are almost as stupid as me and we all need good stories even though we don't know anything anymore. Then the dinner is over and ehe apologizes for not paying my four dollars so as I'm thinking that's a little wierd

All crimes start in the library. Murderers cite their favourites as inspirations for their deeds. If it's Sade, we think to ban it. Or we did. How many massacres are beget by the holy scriptures, THE tome for justification? How many poisoners could cite Agatha Christie?

Let me tell you a story. I read Harold Robbins once. Just once. But I think we'll agree that in this context Robbins is not the pleasure we wish to pursue.

Writing books is like a game. Different books in the different rooms of the house, picked up at different times, pick & mix in one's head, kick starting a story.

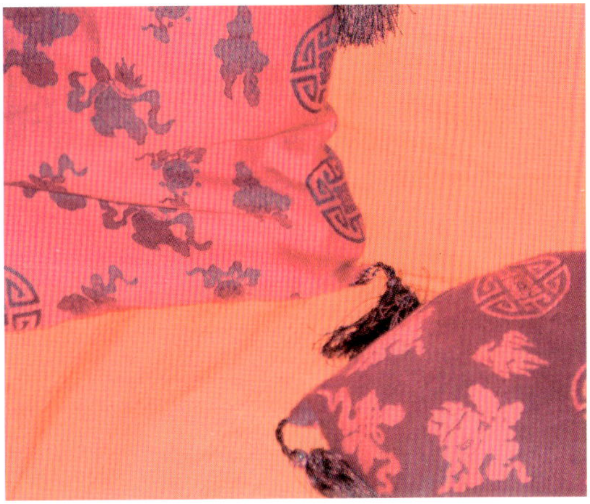

Let's have dinner and discuss it. Are we here to blast away and then kick and make up? Is there any depth to our feelings? Or are we just Playboy bunnies fucking on the hillsides until myxomatosis or mimesis sets in, keels us over?

The problem really is money. I never had the desire for it and I have the desire for it. I want it, mainly to squander, not to live rationally, and yet I don't want it cos it fucks up everyone I meet who has money and then lays everything on the line to lose it. Jewels hanging from my nipples.

I wanted him to rip off my skin, take me away to where I'd always be insane.

Sentences that have no full stop

What do you really want to happen? he asked me. I couldn't answer because I don't reveal the truth to people I know slightly, only to strangers and to people I know well and want to become.

What happens when you have the same dream again and again? Five times let's say.

There's a tyranny at work here, and it wears blue genes (sic). You know I had some of the records before I even met you. Dreaming in the sun and dreaming in the moon. Lovely music. A love of life.

and while I'm still trying to think he says, "I want to relax with you." Of course I don't understand English, then I get it and am very shocked because he insulted my writing we didn't flirt and yet he expects me to stop being frigid. I don't understand how people can act like they're human anymore. Not to mention all this germ warfare going around. So I very carefully and gently explain because I don't want to hurt feelings in case there are such things I'm not human, my emotions are hidden somewhere else and very dangerous, please go away I'm a total catatonia case and catatonia cases are very violent and you shouldn't want to fuck them for fear of explosions. Of course he doesn't understand cause he's a nice rich boy, so he says "I'm so glad you're stopping being a punk.' (I'm dressing very elegantly these days in real black leather and I just got two white silk chairs off my dead grandmother so I'm SOCIETY.() Then I say"how long have you been married?" "Thirteen years," he replies. "Are your wife and you happy?" "We're totally satisfied with each other." "Do you have affairs or one-night stands or both with other women?" "Affairs." "Aren't you scared you might care for another woman more than you care for your wife?" "I could never like another woman as much as I like my wife." Then he proceeds to explain why he's a feminist.

I love society. There's the L+A=N=G=U=A=G=E poets for you and that's why there's no content in their work. Well, don't be nasty now Kathy: you know your opinions are always wrong. This guy just presumed he was going to sleep with me cause I write porn and I didn't even have a choice and he doesn't wear leather. Meanwhile I'm having this wierdo affair with Sylvere (Lotringer) I cancelled twenty dates in a row with him cause I'm such a

At one point we were going to not tell anyone about anything. We were going to form a society, a secret society, go into words, I meant woods, my finger slipped, perhaps sacrifice someone. Gets easier every day to find victims for such a deed. Even those with the right state of mind, not some gullible victim. A whole spiritual sacrifice. But we don't talk about it, never will.

Pure time is not time but a hole, you said. Inside this hole everything that happens does not come back again because it never went away. There is no time; there is.

There is only there is. Is that the key to existence? Does memory bring all into the present? Is my thinking only the present? What comes from the past, or projects into the future, is only the present. There is only now. When I recall, I am not recalling, I am stating the now, where the source is to be found is of no relevance. Only the NOW, the IS. Is that how you feel? So Pip becomes Peter who in turn becomes Pierre. And five hundred thousand soldiers are displayed, raked across the page. Profit the moment.

By profit we mean money. You know why I crave affection, why I sink into the arms of any man who shows me affection. But how can I start talking about my mother? To you, or anyone. I'm a mess of memories, feelings, anxieties. What can I tell you? She was a drunk. It's so embarrassing to admit that, but my mother was a drunk. She'd drink a glass of scotch and fall to the floor, crawl on hands and knees like a dog to the nearest man and set to work on his thigh. No care for whoever was watching. Dad or anyone. Me, for example. Me.

Merry Xmas.

Virginity is only there for the moment. It is not yours to savour. Remember that.

Texts subvert other texts, until what? The music of what? Muzak or life, love of life.

It's no good me remembering any Christmas? I don't do memories. What is there to remember? A Xmas tree? A turkey? Bad TV shows? I don't remember these things. These objects. Perhaps I can remember seeing them. Perhaps I become the turkey. Perhaps I become the tree. Perhaps I'm stuffed. What with? Sage and onion? Or just an onion up my arse? I can see myself

P.S. the "fete" follows - it's turning out to be huge - give me one more week (please)

lobotomy case and I might feel something and of course that is pain then one night, one dark dreary night, he CORNERS me and traps me and after four hours gets me to his loft and of course it's great, so there I am, but the minute I NOTICE him, you know, not just treating him like shit, I'm the shit trouble he says "Oh I hate feelings" "Oh, I want everything to go fast and disappear" (French intonation) so I have to be nastier and cleverer and fool around more than him: it's a great battle; where has love gone...?

fright

Dear Harold Robbins,(

valentines We never knew in the hippie days that you knew more about real politics than Jane Fonda even though you are a little pig.

hatred

I don't know Harold Robbins at all; I do know Sylvere: I can't figure out what he's like and now I might be falling in love with him. Excuse that I'm writing the two of you at the same time; I don't think of you as the same person, but I'm such a lousy letter writer that I want to have mouth diarrhea IMMEDIATELY IMMEDIATELY CONTACT I'M GLAD WE'RE FRIENDS! Your poem Paul is beautiful: all day I've been thinking of <u>interstices</u>,interstices of the night, the grid where (in blackness) you can't percieve connections so everything is the holes of the grid, things just as they are, the holes. I've been reading Husserl lately. Your poem is there: the set-up theatre grids or social perceptions: everyhthting gook mush the holes oh. Oh.

Ocean

fish

I enclose next chapter of GREAT EXPECTATIONS and am glad you like cause it's so dense I think maybe uninteresting except to me and please of course do whatever you want in way of publishing and if there's ever any money GIVE ME LOTS. I NNEEED MINK. I enclose little page FETE too. And my friend Jeffrey Goldberg is putting

Jeffrey Goldberg, 106 Perry St., NYC, NY 100

remembering. I mean I can see myself seeing, not remembering. Remembering does not exist.

Remembering doesn't touch the forgotten.

When one reads work one wrote a number of years ago, one is surprised by it. Was that written by me? I've forgotten it. How good/bad it is. Quite extraordinary. How could I have ever said something like that, or thought that. I can't remember thinking that. Are you sure I wrote it?

This is why we often say not that we remember what it was, but that we remember what it was not.

It's not our memory that continues to grow, but the forgotten. That hole increases in size, though what is within is not known.

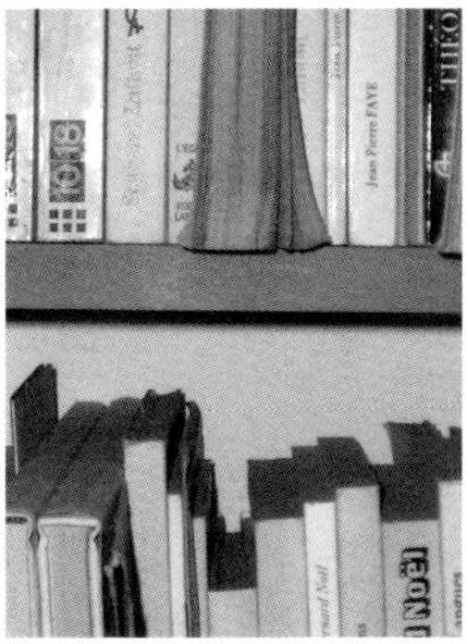

Is that hole a blackness, or a nothing. A blackness is something, for it is black. It is a colour, made up of particles. To say that nothing is visible is untrue. I can see nothing is not true. Unless you think that nothing is visible, comprises particles of something.

When we come up against the forgotten, in mid sentence perhaps, we stand on the abyss. Before us opens a void, an infinity... that forgotten into which we cannot move. We can only retreat and find another path. On that edge language has no future, it spins into a vertigo, the more we try to make it happen, to make it become something. Language has the chance to become madness.

out reprint of NYMPHOMANIAC by me, one by Bokris, and one by Mr. Hell. so maybe after these, I suggest to him last night and he says "Good idea" something by you, two, one, mainly something, cause this is no poetry venture, it's sleazier lower fewer copies poorer, something that got a story, violence, pleasure I need pleasure. Why do I hate talking business? I want to do something for you guys and I love sleaze. Well DO SOMETHING. And say hello to all those nice French friends of yours at CHANGE whom I met. I think James Sherry's through with ROOF. Anyway, he's through. Could you send a copy of IT or ask them to? I'd love to see my crap. I think every word's used over here. No one has any brains anymore. About Iran: I think the Arabs are terrific. I want to hold a pro-Ay... rally. They got a great culture their history book THE MUQUAMMID (lousy spelling) is the most amazing history book I ever read and I think the USA is more disgusting racist than usual but then the businessmen here (the source of this racism spurt) are acting desperate and impolite these days: it's all a hoax and like usual only the poor people are the jokes... Well, that's what I think of Iran, now I'm just another American talking about Iran, as for the Olympics, why doesn't someone come to the East Village and give us fake snow over this garbage so at least we could get some exercise and make use of the piles of dead rats as ski slopes. I think politicians are very unimaginative and besides they don't care enough about their constituencies. Huh. I think it's nice to be nice to your family, I do, especially since mine's dead. I'd loved your letter; it made me feel good all over, sitting on the subway to SEMIOTEXT(E) party, smiling

I never dedicate anything to anyone but, maybe, I don't know yet cause it aint written, next chapter of GREAT EXPECTATIONS under-worlds for you - no more room- no more talk- no more communication, lo

Oh this guy's doing a book of mine in Holland & bringing me to Europe around June so I'LL SEE YOU THEN!! It seems pretty definite —

love K-

Dear Sylvère,

Shit, I forgot what I wanted to write to tell you. Later then. Luxe

Do you want to hear a patronizing story, how we reinforce the idea of second-class status on those not from our superior countries. At the school of both girls, each Xmas, they ask students to prepare a shoebox of gifts to be sent as a present to children in other countries, whether Eastern Europe, Africa… I suspect. With the rider, from one teacher, perhaps others, that the children fill the box with things they don't want, their cast-offs, junk from their drawers. Instead of saying, think how much you have, material things, money, use a bit of that money to go out & purchase afresh for these children. No, give them cast offs, something is better than nothing for those who have nothing.

Kathy's name was not Acker. Anyway. So what's with changing names.

I was horny. I'm still incredibly horny.

The first fuck with someone usually shatters me: I'm real nervous cause I'm scared the person'll think I'm a lousy fuck I want to do anything to please the person I have to figure how I can come hard and lots. The second time we fuck is best: I'm not so frenzied I'm no longer in love I've figured how to come I'm not yet bored. From then on it's downhill: I become more and more bored.

But I can cast my mind back, if I crawl out your window, I will meet the real people of the neighbourhood, find Melvyn down there relating. He tries to slow everything down, he doesn't want life to go too quickly. As he approaches the end of the book, he savours every word to hold off that moment when he reaches the end. It was a good book. Now all he has are the ghosts of the characters living within. He wants to live in that book forever. Daphne, he pleads. Daphne, will you join me.

I have learned what art really is. Art is not in some far-off place.

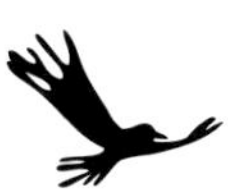

RESOURCES

I Dreamt I was a Nymphomaniac Imagining: The Black Tarantula (Kathy Acker)
Star Jaws: Peter Gordon
Great Expectations: Kathy Acker
The Book of the Forgotten: Bernard Noël (trans Paul Buck & Glenda George)
Physical writing: feeling: Melvyn Freilicher
Extracts from a life: Lydia Davis

K -

Today for once I've got plenty of time to write to you - I'm sitting for an artist. I thought he was trying to pick me up - we met in a bar and he asked me 'If I pay a hundred will you stay all night?' When he explained, he was so perfectly easy in his manner that I felt free from embarrassment, and agreed. He made a little speech of thanks and took my arm and bore me off to his house, where he uses the library as a studio.

My hair is pinned up and there's a silver gauzy wrap around my shoulders. He makes me hold it spread wide under my breasts, displaying them, bare apart from two strings of pearls. Like Cora. Doesn't he know anything about clothes?

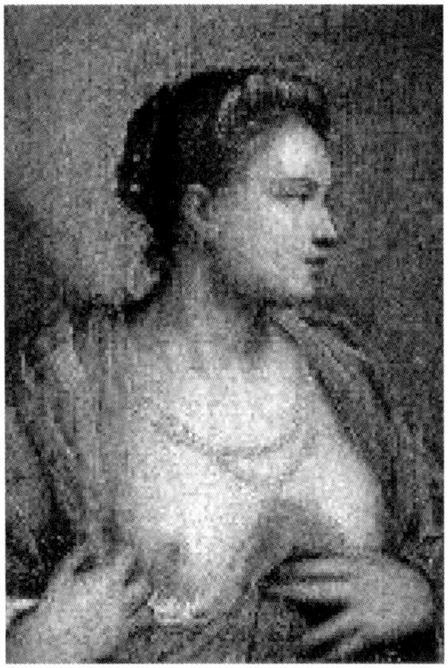

"No whore living in Venice may dress in, or wear on any part of her person, gold, silver or silk, except for her coif, which may be of pure silk; and such women may not wear necklaces, pearls, or rings with or without stones, either in their ears or in any other imaginable place."

I'm watching his long,

tenacious fingers apply the paint in thick wodges, like butter. I think if I were to dip my finger in I would retch just from the feel of it. I drank some coffee an hour ago and now I have a bitter taste in my mouth but he said I can't get up yet.

When I shuffle in my chair he looks at me like he wants to rip off my skin. I'm not naked enough for him. There's a curious something that settles over you when you're naked and posing. You're veiled. Sitting like this I'm not myself, and that not-myselfness clothes me - he can't see me. To do that he would have to fix me to a cross or a wheel, flagellate me, flay me - strip my skin off bit by bit until he bared the skull beneath.

Still I'm sitting here day-dreaming. Looking at his thin hands. Those with thin fingers may have large tools, but there is no test other than the ocular.

He wants my profile now, so I can look out of the window as I write. If I saw you standing at the sill, beckoning and re-beckoning to me - even if I thought you were roaming out there somewhere, I'd prove I were your friend. I'd crawl out. Oh Kathy, Kathy, do come to Europe. Oh, do - ONCE more!

Daphne

My Dear Bucks and Georges, well three performances down the drain
and 400 in the bank account until the next clothes frenzy, always
luxury before necessity, that's our motto, my motto: I'm just schizped-
and everyone liked the performances except of course for all the people
whose names I mentioned in the texts and they should all go to hell
except Sylvere speaking of Sylvere. Oh Glenda that sounds so good a
book of letters let's be real disgusting the machos aren't even being
guilty anymore. Oh yes (I AM schizo today actually it's just my back
it's a mess from Sylvere) and I've got all all this shit work and not
doing it, writing you instead cause mmmmwah!, in and out of the
parentheses (just like sex these days) where was I/? where I am? I
mean my mind is shot, I keep listening to Marianne Faithfiul and I
met these people from NEW MUSICAL EXPRESS at my performance: all do
you know them? (in and out without parentheses) all I mean to say my
head is gone cause this thing with Sylvere keeps getting I don't
know what it's getting of course it's not ROMANCE or ANY WORD cause
I'm a cripple and he's so tough - so much for fantasies - but meanwhile
I might end of dead and not from extasy though extasy sure goes
along with it. I walk into the gym to work out and the women STARE
at my back but they're much too bourgeois to open their mouths an
or close their endless fashion gossip and I love it. Fuck the
scared capitalists. Maybe I will end up dead. But this I don't know
if it's lovely and who cares S&M doesn't go beyond the bed unlike
the usual relationships where it's all S&M outside the bed and
shit inside, just like my dear husband Mr. Gordon who just phoned
me how dare I mention REAL NAMES during my performances especially
his girl friend's cause her twat is sacred and don't I have any
respect in me. Oh a new book's out and it's on the way to you!!!!
No, I have no respect. I hate pain and will cry out. Friends friends
friends. It's very good here now. I'm a little worrried about the
thing with Sylvere cause it's so good but will worry more about
new chapter: all porn. Oh also gonna begin a terrorist

press with some Italians. Again porn & politics. Life OK now IT'S SPRING. IS Spring

Sounds good about your mother—
Oh what's happening?
I tell everyone I know 400 2
Love - Kathy

Now is the time to go out & buy new clothes. Shall I just buy those French labels, or a suit with lapels, something snazzy? Anything to get me one stitch closer to Europe, all those countries stitched together. Knitted clothes. I love knitted clothes. Until I get bored with them.

I'd rather get bored with clothes and all that stuff than bored with what happens in my real life, in my home, my body, my bed. Always to spread wide my intimacy instead of life. Why do I do that? **ONE DAY THEY'LL BOUND AND GAG ME.**

What you have to beware of is the past that keeps stamping itself in the present. Or the gin that trades under other names. Blows its own tune. Becomes a lawyer, changes its gender as it shifts across the drafts. Or just… shits.

You see, Paul, the real issue is emotion. It scares me because I'm so fucked up.

How can I perform and not talk about my real world? Am I supposed to be a fake in bed too? So don't tell me what I can do and what I can't do. If you want to go lay some other cunt that's your prerogative, but leave me to my cocks. Thank you.

Oh dear, this is grave, I need to get the accent right. Kinda cute. Do I have to hear that often? Or is it my fault that I keep blurting it out when I mean to swallow it. Oh dear. Let's talk Italian and I'll only think about terrorists… until saturation. Wet, I like being wet.

All this has to be done under test conditions. If you still have one erection, I can't start the next until your erection is down. So I want you to tell me the names of the people you hate. You mean, hate today? Today. Tomorrow. People you love then. Same thing, probably. Just name names. Why? Because if I just let you sit there you might start fantasizing. What's wrong with fantasizing? A lot of fantasizing comprises rebel behaviour. Right. So I say suppress. Why would I want to suppress? Because you might get into an awful lot of trouble otherwise. You have to know when to suppress and when not to suppress. You just can't be out of control. You're not a kid any longer.

(((Magnolias. I always adored magnolias.)))

I love looking at magnolias whereas I don't like looking at cameras that are looking at me. Or yes, I do like it if the photographer is right. All I

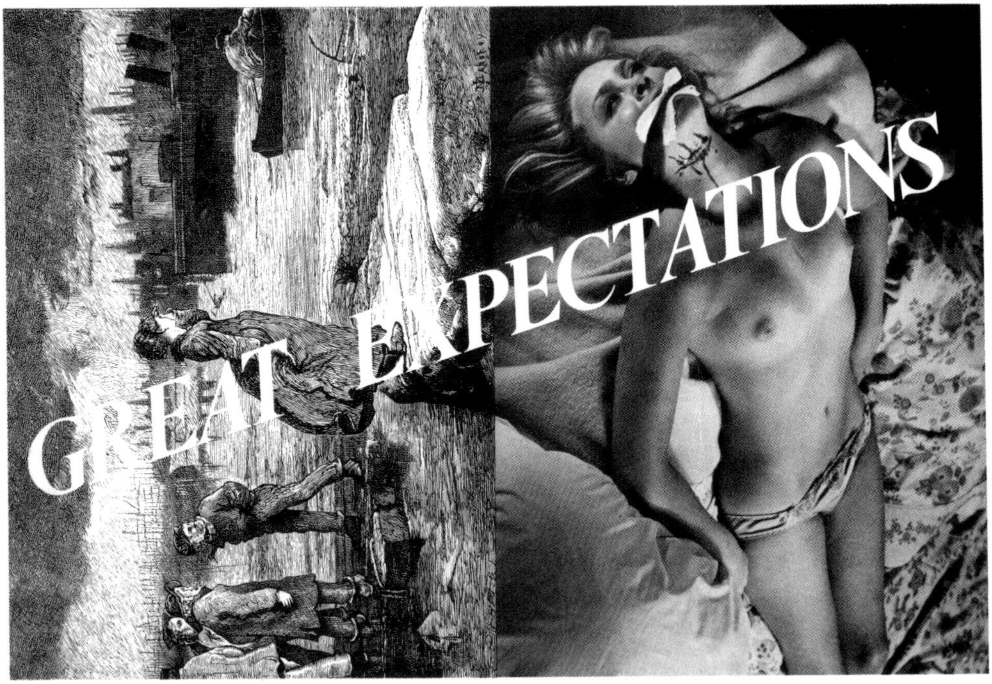

KATHY ACKER

Visuals by DIEGO CORTEZ

"*I Dreamt I Was Nymphomaniac*" a new book from Traveller's Digest Publications

A Performance

March 11-12, 8:30pm

THE KITCHEN

484 Broome Street

think about is myself behind my face, looking through the windows of my eyes, imprisoned.

How does one know what to write about? Only the critic writes about things that give no pleasure. I only write about things that I can attach my ideas to. Art does not have to "pay me". What a terrible phrase. And thought. It doesn't even have to touch me personally. Isn't pleasure enough? It can do other things too, but one of the great beauties of art is that it's an instrument of pleasure. After all, pleasure can be quite a rarity in one's life.

How terrible to be blind and have to dictate one's writing. The pleasure of writing is the need to be able to see what is written, so that it can be read and rewritten, worked with, upgraded, edited. I have to be able to reread.

To hear those words, "Susan, I'm a writer, not a reader," would cut right through me, even if I understood it came from a writer in his twilight years. Rather the thought of the pleasure of reading, the pleasure that perhaps one might lose oneself in the reading. What joy to become the other. The whirlpool of identity. The vertiginous textual world of I Kathy, I Paul, I Daphne.

RESOURCES
Florida: Kathy Acker
Great Expectations: Kathy Acker
Overexposed: Sylvère Lotringer
Where the Stress Falls: Susan Sontag
Interview: On Art and Consciousness: Susan Sontag

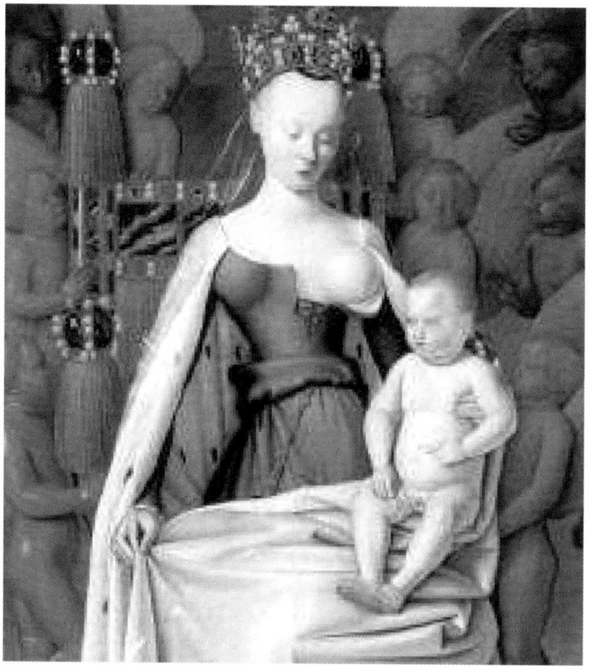

I'm posing again, so you get a postcard. Still sitting here promising pneumatic bliss, but not to anyone close at hand. Actually my hands are free just now, as he's painting my hair.

He's quite proud, he twined beads and clips in it and managed to tame it for once. So while he concentrates on the empty shell of me I let my eyes – but not my head – roam the room. On the table there's a jam-jar full of lilacs that I can't quite smell. A cracked mirror just behind him shows me to myself, suspended as it were, like a spider in the centre of a crystal net.

Through it I look at him, looking back at the woman on the canvas who is not me. The limbs he adjusts only translate something already inside him. He may make reference to my form, but he is penetrated by an image that he will bring forth into the light. Here, with a man I do not know, I fling away restraint and modesty: his vanity requires no response from me and this frees me.

341 East 5th St. #4

New York, NY 10003

Dear P & G- Oh, I know I should write you two separately cause you ARE TWO PEOPLE (are people people?? you are people I know that) I just got up to get another cup of tea and forgot everything. Well- anyway- thank god the mind is the most unstable....I am about to go to California and North for a month (a tour, and of course I'll return with no matter money is matter money? I am REALLY DAZED TODAY) and want to write you as soon as possible: I will be at Lebel's festival in June, I arrive Brussels June 9 (can't make it earlier cause I only return from California middle of May and can't over-exert myself, will discuss... oh the Brontes'!) O.K. so Paris by noon or so May no June, what is a name, 10 (This letter is definitely based on mistakes: is that a theory of language?) I love the Clash they're on the radio now, but after that festival... Shall I visit England when you return? I have to go to Holland for a few days (3 days) and after that am free, except... Except I've been very sick lately (PID again) and this time am not recovering fast enough, a bad case of overwork I fear, I've forbidden myself writing for a few weeks to recover, I am just not recovering very well- the problem is the weaker the body gets, the better the writing comes- and the affair with Sylvere was no hope: a little too much S&M and or pain and a little too little compassion. I think I'm going dyke. Though right now I'm not going anything cause NYPHOMANIAC just came out and everyone loves it and social social social more work I love work but I am so worn down, dear, I might as well be in the 19th century and have tuberculosis: it was much more romantic back then. Is that this what Women's Lib has done: transformed romantic TB into workaday

When Kathy lands in England she is scared, because she don't know anybody, nobody is there to meet her, and she don't speak the language. Estuary is very particular. Out of customs she is hit on by men, each tries to inveigle her into his car. They call them taxis, but she's not so sure. They look like rip-offs. She just wants to reach the centre. Expect to breakdown.

Everywhere she goes people come on to her. It's not a matter of skin colour, or degree of poverty. They all want a piece of her arse. At first she's worried she'll be raped, so she complies, spreads wide. She doesn't feel love, so it's okay. She can fuck without reasoning.

MARRIAGE DIVORCE MARRIAGE DIVORCE. That's all they could talk about as they fucked each other.

I like to lose myself in sex as in books as in paintings. To lose myself in contemplation of many things. Contemplation and the ability to lose oneself in what one choices is an orgasm in itself, an orgasm by another name. An abandonment that is a transformation, an equating with the other.

Perhaps it's only in films, or in our readings of bad literature, forms that pursue clichés that we find orgasm always always always has to be the release of a cry, a scream, a piercing shriek. Does one shriek to inform the other, assuming the other is present and the orgasm is not reached as a solitary experience? How many times does it happen quietly, even in silence? Concentration can be so extreme, the passion so deep that one comes to the edge of orgasm with the most minimal activity. I remember Liz being so impassioned, even in minimal foreplay, that a slight and fractional breath of air in her ear was dynamic enough to trigger her orgasm.

And the sound of the piano. It can break my concentration where a violin or cello can't. Kathy had asked me to note the dates of her availability, asked me to note the dates when she would be away, and where she would be, visiting various friends, asking me to note their telephone numbers as well, just in case I should need to contact her, for what reason I didn't actually know, but people like to run through their itinerary and make sure you can get them at any time and place, knowing that the likelihood is most unlikely. It

no love stress and exhaustion and a SEMIOTICIAN telling me I am a masochist and will never escape my fate? I think I'll be a masochist in writing only. Is that the same as in name only. I've got a new message: EXTASY KILLS. I dun wanna die, mommy. Mommy died. I'll read THE GOLDEN BOUGH again. The mind works so fast! I just finished letter telling Stonehill if BLOOD AND GUTS isn't out by 10/1/80 I'm doing it, so come what may, it'll appear by Christmas so it will be a merry BLOOD AND GUTS Christmas and I'm very happy that's all resolved. See: no masochism, daddy. Oh, I'll get down to business. Oh, I'm reading Eliot and Auden. I am having a nervous breakdown. And I love them! (except for very late Eliot: he DID get simplistic). I never knew you were a movie star, Paul! I am drobling over the cover of HONEYMOON MOONERS. I want a copy! Yum! Haven't heard from Mr. Alexander yet. (My maiden name, adopted, is Alexander.) Can't find the DEADMAN. Will try harder. Will write Riverside before leaving but since won't be back to get mail till 5/15, maybe not enough time? Would LOVE to read with you. Will also write Faye, etc. and if I am lame and late, am just terribly overworked: have been a good girl for so long, all these performances etc., now must be a baby and GET WELL. Very anxious mind. OK. maybe if I send Faye the GREAT EXPECTATIONS snd he uses what he wants? Or should he consult with you? My address in SF can get me through there until 5/14 is 80 Langton St., SF, Ca. 94103. Am going to write you and write you until ARTFORUM calls up for that dinner they're taking me out to tonight anywhere I want (HEE HEE I wish I felt better). I love Iris. My Rosucrucian friend says I get over PID (Venus problem) by ascending to the next

maintains the lifeline, a rope of flowers. Instead it gave me a list of contacts, all new to me, whom I found myself contacting, and indeed visiting at later dates, an ever-increasing circle of women who were to give me what Proust calls "moments of pleasure". Remembering now, I did not seem to think there were very many. But when I thought it over again, reclining on the sofa, the names returned. I counted that *a dozen conferred on me their ephemeral favours*. And then later another came to me. Thinking on that number, that baker's dozen of thirteen, I started to slice and butter them, one on top of each other, and recall that I'd forgotten the very first, the one who'd set me off on that road. Kathy herself. She made it fourteen.

What do you say to more emphasis on context than on content? Or to just producing work as commercial product, no other use whatsoever?

To walk with the text, to give con-text to it. To change the con-text.

I would have suggested to you to walk. Walk. Don't walk. How to put it? Declaring the opposites in alternation in order to invent what you are thinking.

You chose to fight. Who are you to leave us? In this room where you are speaking. I do not hear. What are you saying in the smells of the restaurant? To live but I understand to die. To leave. Let's leave. There is no memory. No departing. We have passed. Words I do not want yes. Words these words there are no words.

You will speak in a book. Don't write cry. There is no sickness. It's a book in which I say nothing where you say the words. These words I destroyed these words.

I WILL NEVER SWALLOW YOUR SPERM. I FEEL NOTHING BUT DISGUST FOR THE WORDS COMING FROM YOUR MOUTH. FILTH. I WISH YOU WOULD DROP DEAD, RIGHT HERE, BEFORE ME. THEN I WOULD BE CAPABLE OF CRYING. AFTERWARDS. WHEN I WOULD BE RID OF YOU. CRY. THIS VERY INSTANT I WANT TO KILL YOU. ALL YOUR FRIENDS WILL BE THERE. IT WILL BE MY GREATEST ROLE NEXT TO YOUR COLD BODY. I HAD ASKED YOU TO BRING ME MAGNOLIAS AND YOU FORGOT. THIS VERY INSTANT I SHOULD HAVE SCREAMED AND REFUSED TO GO ON LIVING. I SHOULD HAVE SWALLOWED YOUR MOUTH.

Perhaps I would not speak. Saying nothing as in a dream, for too many voices would spread my lips apart and then the blackness would come. And, urged by you, by your silence, by your eyes, and your body which would make as

house which is the sun. Oh Lemaire. He hates me now. He's making sure Le Seuil won't do TARANTULA cause he says "I'm too hard to translate" and I don't know about Bourgois: the contract I have with them says BLOOD AND GUTS has to come out by end of 1981 or I take back [redacted] is so off me, he really [redacted] RSE WORSE POMPOUSPOM [redacted] pomposity I mean it's [redacted] lation cause I hate that creep (Oh dear, this letter can never be published: sexual gossip is always public but THIS is PRIVATE) I have wonderful stories about [redacted] Italy with no money and 24 [redacted] made it back to him and said. [redacted] ks away, etc. May we all stay away from business and egotistic extasy. Am very touched that Wilkinson dedicated his piece to me; the review was off; I kind of have a policy to disregard what people say about my books cause it's always so coocoo, but I'm getting a little bugged at to what extent people don't see that KATHY GOES TO HAITI is a take-off on Nancy Drew plus stable porn: a genre piece, and therefore not simple, not really a novel at all: meant to be extreme of what the "20th century" novel is: psychology etc. so of course there's narrative etc. I mean the problems are in capital letters and erased that way (not by hippie repression) just as now WE all flaunt our PSYCHOSES: UNDERLINE DON'T CHANGE there is no change everything just as it is. Even dumb stupid fake novels pretending

if to leave, I would say to you: "I am not speaking, because my life does not resemble me." We are lost inside.

I don't know what I want. My want keeps running ahead to be here where nothing is wanting but you. Who do not want. Who does not want? I make you he, object out there to see so seeing you I can be clear. Of want? You are not here to see.

Art is the fashion I wear on my back. On my feet. To cut my teeth on.

Artists unheard of three years ago are commanding $40,000 a painting—prices it used to take artists a whole career to arrive at. Once, the idea of art historical importance stabilized the market value of an artist's work, but prices no longer reflect this—how could they? Now they reflect speculation on short-term market scarcity. However, there may be problems in paradise. Sales at those prices are either between dealers (who don't seem to keep the work for very long) or to, well, people who know little about art and take the dealers' advice on à la mode investments. At those prices people get nervous, and when somebody else becomes chic, the newly arrived will unload (since their relationship to the work is superficial to begin with) and prices will most probably come crashing down. The pity is that all this has very little to do with the art; certainly very little to do with the artist's relationship to his or her work. But in the end it does because such pressure makes it very difficult for artists to go in the direction that their work is taking them. In such a situation there isn't sufficient time for the work to be evaluated on its own terms and establish its own meaning. How many of us can be unaffected in our evaluation of work that got too hot too fast and then too cold too fast? When a work goes from $40,000 to, say, $8,000, will we still be able to see the ideas of the artist, or will we be looking instead at lapels too wide—or simply at 'failure'? **I think there is a certain responsibility of the artist to fight for the meaning of her or his work.**

RESOURCES

Kathy Goes to Haiti: Kathy Acker
The Sexual Life of Catherine M.: Catherine Millet (trans Adriana Hunter)
Cities of the Plain: Marcel Proust (trans C.K.Scott-Moncrieff)
Impassioned with Some Song We: Kathy Acker
Us These Photographs, No: Mathieu Bénézet (trans Dominic Di Bernardi)
Here & there: Daphne Marlatt
Necrophilia, Mon Amour: Joseph Kosuth

to be real. KATHY GOES TO HAITI really is a nasty little machine and I shouldn't complain when machines react to machines I mean I set it up and no one ever needed understanding anyway is that what the mind's about? What's the mind about? What are you talking about girl? Dear Glenda, this isn't a very womanly letter: my sex is sick and I think I'm a neutral. YOU'RE WRITING PROSE YOU'RE WRITING PROSE! You and Daphne Marlatt are my two magic woman writers cause you allow yourselves to be female and you WRITE! I read Virginia Woolf again, but you are not sloppy as she sometimes is (she indulges and, unlike Auden, who everytime he can step steps in the most precise meaning complicated way he can) she often slipshods and is simplistic). You are not and yet you remain delicate. Is that true fivolity? I am one big question but I can only ask through other texts: I hardly have a language of my own. I've been reading THE COCKTAIL PARTY which allows me that question: I AM in my thirties and want that recognition, or rather, that question: I want to go OUT in that Western way (as opposed to my Hindu teacher) of using images to get to another way: THE LANGUAGE. Is this understandable? When I really try to speak, I invent the language. Are you using Elmer or is Elmer using you? But I don't think writing has to be based on this disintegration of the body. Or maybe I'm just playing scaredy-cat. There are not enough women writers now. I keep thinking thiaS Again and again. We have to get tough meaning get unneurotic chance the way the men did. No more flowers, only our ways: delicacy, whatever. Through Eliot am going to Jessie L. Weston. Thinking of seeing you two again makes me happy- there's here's the phone

All my lovelovelove

Kat

baby

Kathy

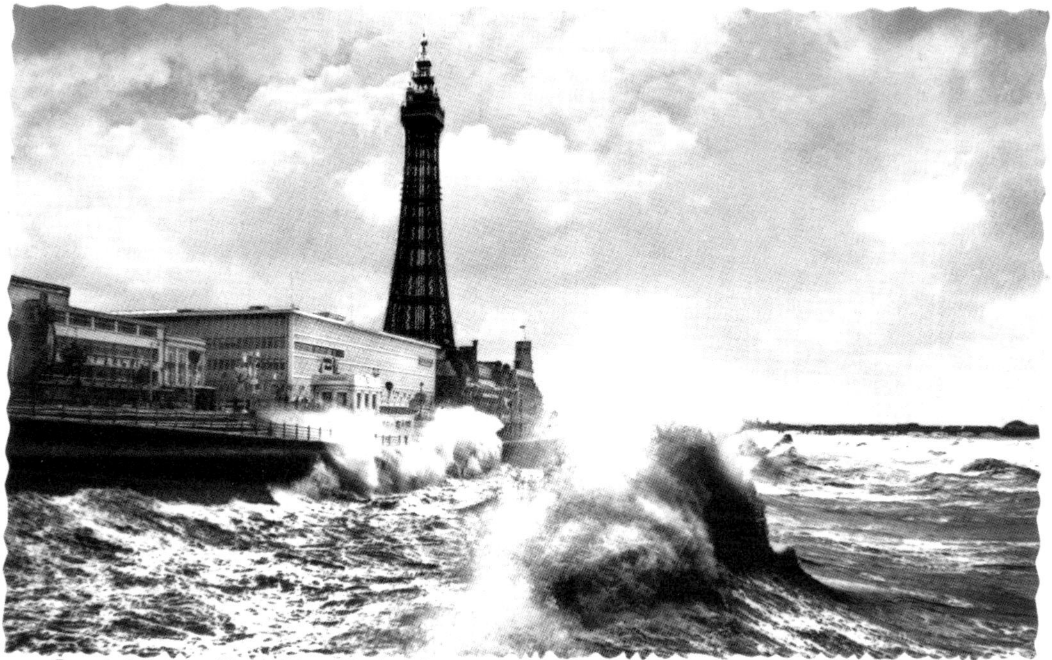

Rough Sea from North Pier, Blackpool. ET.4314

Nov 12 dear Paul & Glenda

By BAMFORTH & CO. LTD. PUBLISHERS. HOLMFIRTH. Yorks

Just to say (again) that Bill F.! keeps telling me he wants to do the tape with you, K. Acker & someone French whose name escapes me. I suggest you plan to make it over Xmas when he is not teaching & that you get him to finalise it NOW. O xxx Sus

NOTTING HILL W.11 2 - PM 12 NOV 1980

Printed in Spain

Paul Buck / Glenda George
4 Bower Street
Maidstone
Kent

Susan Hiller

Dear Paul and Glenda, Have been in total mess, total hell getting out of NYC, or rather, seeing what hell NYC is: can't find people to pack my stuff even for money cause kitchen roof caves in, LITERALLY, then everyone's so scared of getting ripped off cause everyone now in NYC is ripping each other off nothing happens no one will do anything without money up front and meanwhile my NYC bank refuses to transfer money, even though that's illegal, and all the mail is fucked up cause no one is doing anything where is CURTAINS? I'm DYING not dying except in sexi sexual to see, oh oh oh, oh oh oh, and besides NYC slipping into the chasm.... So still don't have books to send you another copy of NYMPHO and Jeffrey's no longer talking to me cause I'm living in Seattle with a MAN so there go those royalties, why do writers become celibate?, will do my damndest am trying to get another copy, if you do recieve, send notice cause I don't think I'll ever get books again (at least for six months till Jeffrey sees how STUPID and PETTY he's being: I can't (keep) going around being faithful to a man I'm not fucking and will never fuck cause I like him but the idea of fucking him, ugh pu-wee, and besides, besides everything besides the world, I'm in love: this one's rough too cause I am definitely not used to sharing anything with anyone, but he's a good man, goddamnit he works as a teamster (one of the strongest unions here USA) and yesterday Carter announced in the summer the Teamsters- trucking's going to be deregulated which means, in effect, no more union - destroys one of the strongest unions in this country - and a quarter of the truckers will be out of work. Things wierd in this country; slow realization that there's heavy ecommomic downfalling ahead turns people here right-wing, hatred of minorities, looks like Reagan's gonna be President, everyone scared, crazy.... We plan to move to Europe by December. But things good out here; am seeing slowly how fucked up I've been NYC years: no more normal person, media jetset hype faster faster, no sense of what a person is, everything out of fear opposite considered normal until the

I'm generous. I'll give you nothing.

Emptiness formed within her.

Her shoes squelched in the mud and the rain drenched her.

But trembling gave her pleasure.

Taking his hand put it between her thighs.

They danced an indecent arse-grasp rhumba.

Again she said.

No one could answer.

Suck her off.

She pulled the mouth of the patron to her and opened the abyss of her lips to its decay.

He stopped dead, rubbing his hands together.

Mary climbed onto the bench…

She splashed urine over herself with her hands.

They took up positions around the victim.

Gripped by a distressing happiness which opened into emptiness.

She squatted and shat on the vomit.

She remained violent.

Wretchedly naked.

The study of beauty is a duel in which the artist cries out in terror before being vanquished

vicious cycle, fear increasing, NYC the best example, doesn't make Baudelaire but a robot. Hard and uncomfortable to un-robotize. But when can see, love, beyond my paranoia know it's O/K/ Reading Hemingway Fitzgerald Anselm Hollo. Can read poetry again and love it! Not just feel jealousy and speed! And a week ago climbed a mountain, didn't get to top, but reached glacial lake snow all up from sun ocouldn't believe I had done that, absolutely incredible. Going down there are ice caves, across the sound paths through rain forest like a house, a dwelling, the beach. Geography like words in paragraph. Writing, shit life of Baudelaire, always back to him, end of Georges Sand. How was festival? Am sure I'm in every one's black book for not going. Except for M. Gerard- George Lemiare: recieved a letter from him, first in six months, telling me it's very UNPROFESSIONAL of me to read in France before I've got a book published and without his permiss[illegible] and he's still my friend!!!!! Wish I could have done plauy with [illegible] u. How did it go? [illegible] ??? Turns out with all the moving NYC problems [illegible] totally flat so no way I could have g[illegible] [illegible]e and do this Seattle thing a[illegible] [illegible]d Logie (the guy) really is wonderful. Yes, G., [illegible] I've change[illegible] my life; is mortality no fun more fun, excuse me, ? No. I'm totslly freaked out. I'm always fre[illegible]ked out. But the robot language isn't a viable one. And the writing's going well. Gotta see about new languages. So great, P., to hear about all your stuff being published. Wow. I WANT HONEYMOON KILLERS/ Like I want to eat. I eat lots these days. Think I'm pregnant. Back to cheapo three dollar herb abortion. Hope it works. I hate being fat. Speaking of HONEYMOON KILLERS....So am learning to read French better and IRIS, you see now everyone here is angry at me cause I've deserted NYC and fame and fortune and back-knifing and all my old lousy boyfriends they're the ones really angry at me but they also had the publisheing power.... Never stick with a girl. I Ideas of serials are great: people will get more and more excited, build-up, I'm going back to publishing my own stuff, the more self-control the better, Stonehill is now

trying to take all this sex out of BLOOD AND GUTS IN HIGHSCHOOL so I think I'm going to get this new lawyer to take book away from them & do it myself (I already have typesetting) before December. I HATE PUBLISHERS. Only POETS POETS should be allowed to live! God am I moody. Seattle's an empty hole - almost no expressions - we live off a hot plate, no bathroom. I'm too old to be a punk & I'm happy. Hemingway's a fucking good writer - love, K—

You see you bust your head against a wall. Where are you going to find love? How can you run away from yourself? Passion collects. You want the mountains and the peaks, you want the river to flow and the ice to melt. You want the precipice and the abyss. You want the fault line that has no fault. You want the strata without reason. You want the bed without seams. You want the quilt without stains. You want to be fucked and loved. You want to escape and be there. You want safety and risk. You want to come forever. You want to find paradise on earth. You want to be. Just be. I be. You is.

How do I get out of here? A stone is thrown at her. "Why d'you throw a stone at me?" He throws another. "Cos I want you to die." She cries. Then she is told she has to fight back. Otherwise there is no respect for her. "I'm going to kill you if you do that again," she says. He smiles, then laughs. He takes her hand. He is happy. There are tears in his eyes.

RESOURCES

Great Expectations: Kathy Acker
The Deadman: Georges Bataille (trans Paul Buck)
Twenty Prose Poems: Charles Baudelaire (trans Michael Hamburger)
Kathy goes to Haiti: Kathy Acker

THE PROCESS

(Eostur-Monath MMIV)

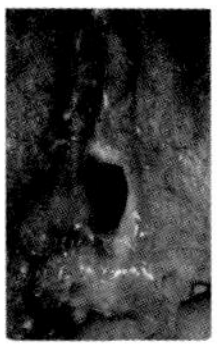

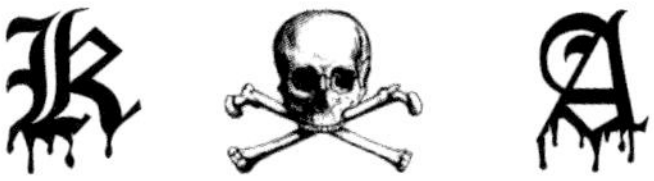

Live and Ill from The Filthy Womb of Blood

Monday 5th April

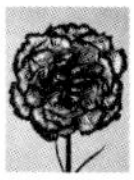

IRREVERSIBLE POSSESSION

'Oestrus is an irrational drive: Plato, Laws, 854b:
"My good man, the evil force that now moves you and prompts you to go temple-robbing is neither of human origin nor of divine, but it is some impulse bred of old in men from ancient wrongs unexpiated, which courses round wreaking ruin; and it you must guard against with all your strength"'.

I slot the cartridge in to the machine and hear the sound of the tape being chewed. I try another. It's the same for all the tapes.
The VCR is dying. Gotta get a new one today and fast.
Or the process is fucked before it's even started.

[Opening Scene: shadow puppet murder, screams, a lace table-cloth, bloody knife falls to the floor, a child's shiny black shoes, a Christmas tree, sound of a demented nursery rhyme].

'Cool' jazz in the crypt. Bandleader, Marc Daly, son of Mary,
complains the music is too traditional. He reminds the band
that the music came out of the bordellos,
like the one on Rue de L'Echiquier.

Cut to 'Congresso di Parapsychology', the camera pans to
RED CURTAINS then passes through.
The voice over reminds us that telepathy is not restricted to superior species but also to
butterflies, termites and Zebras, Zebras, Zebras.
The moon is reflected in a pool of piss. Water flows through the cave beneath the watchtower
where Francis, Kathy and a young red-haired girl attend Lillith.
The cave is draped in webs. Kathy wears a black lace veil across her face.
According to witchfinders who bang their drums above
SHE must be a succubus...a sex demon who lies below...
But how could a daughter of Lillith like K be a supplicant? –
she is a transvestite pirate incubus,
the jewels they have taken from the patriarchs hang from her nipples.

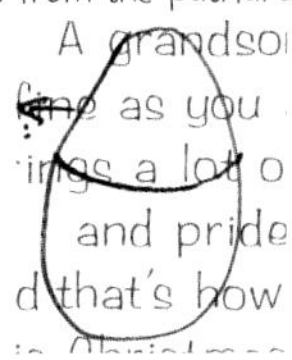

The image of the egg forms a heart then divides.

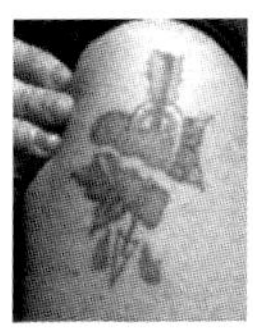

Signora Helga Ulman, addresses the Congress. "I have to make it clear that my powers have nothing to do with magic. I can sense thoughts the moment they occur. Some I can even sense a long time afterwards. They are so strong they remain attached to rooms like cobwebs and the threads of the spider queens who keep their victim slashed and bound in silk, still alive, to suck their life at leisure. It was believed in ancient times that the Spider Woman could control the movement of the sun with her web. At one sitting of the accursed Wilton Way Circle that I attended words began to fragment, each of us began speaking the same butchered tongue, a spiralling thread of syllabic gibberish passing through all our mouths at once, drawing the image closer, and closer, the image of The Supplice, coming to fill the space of the black window. The image feeds our minds eye like a spider's prey. We four became the spider. 8 legs 8 eyes".

"Psychic reception is not coherent", Helga Ulman continues, "It does not fit in to any narrative-cognitive sequence. Psychic communication is lateral, incoherent, like K's writing... 'Stylistically: simultaneous contrasts, extravagancies, incoherencies, half-formed misshapen thoughts, lousy spelling, what signifies what? What is the secret of this chaos?' It occurs *through* time like déjà vu. When one is visited by a ghost in filthy rags or a premonition (a ghost from the future) one is no longer IN TIME. It kicked in immediately when I read this text for the second time, no delay... the egg... the cream oval upon which the CUNT which is the world was to bleed...I searched for an image online... scrolled down the page of images and deja-vu kicked in hard... A sinister echo of the coming *grand mal*...immediate reco(i)llection...so I cut back straight into the text...couldn't wait...shot my head-load all over your hard-boiled egg.

This is what I wrote in Barcelona, the day after I read K's letters for the first time, Carol showed me the best of her porn collection and Carmela had to be locked in the cellar:

Sometimes blood flows
through the crenulations
in the broken surface
of the white oval
and the dying mud
crawls between her toes
and plants squeeze into land
where the fresh creak meets the sound

Perhaps I have opened the same search page before. That was certainly the feeling. I had been there before...there was the egg...the association...the cellar...the sound of Carmela pissing through the locked door...then I typed in the search...I was sitting here, in this very spot. I was thinking whether or not I should begin writing into *Spread Wide* before I had read the whole thing...how I could not begin as soon as I began...I had already scanned through the text...had picked up fragments...Troppman was strong...already the back drop of my thoughts was set before 'the racecourse watchtower'...the place where K has been mapped in a cluster hub with *L'Abbe C* and the Shining Twins...I was there already...and then I hit the page...

There was the usual arrangement of images. The first I recognized was an infernal self-portrait of Tapiés from the 1950's. I scanned left, down, right...some maps...an image of some men sitting at a table. I scan down lower and that's when it hit...sudden sinister rush of déjà vu...looking for the egg...but instead I saw...

I felt fear as I saw...an aura of being here before...frozen...wanting to hold on...like being in the presence of a ghost...terrified but knowing you may never have the opportunity to commune with this spirit again... you want to hold it and yet not see what you sense in the peripheries of your vision...a white sheet flapping from a window...the presence of the spirit out of time...the revenant...and this revenant was female...the sense of a dark female memory...relational...someone I had known and loved in the past...it was an other person...a definite sense of another person...a lover...the painful memory of past lover. Now I will try to go there again..."

Helga Ulman closes her eyes and grasps the hands of the paranormalists at her sides.

"It's gone. The egg's not there. But there was something...I can't explain it. Something strange...Like a knife entering flesh... There!" she recoils violently and thuds her head against the wall, "I feel it again. It's here...I sense death. I feel...a presence. I have entered into contact with a perverse mind. Its thoughts are of death! I heard this twisted thought, cruel and childish at the same time"

Consciousness cuts camera-like a sound instant from here to here to here to here. It's a telecom thing. Consciousness in multiple places at once. Fantomas knows. "I am floating on water, I am propped against a bar. I am everywhere". The cinematographer turns us all into prototelepaths. Can we predict the future? Will our terrible expectations come true, or will it be even worse? (As we observe a disease, so we catch it and give it lodging in ourselves. Is it a surprise then that the imagination should bring fevers and death to those who allow it free play and encourage it? (Montaigne)). The whodunit-occult-mystery plot is an exercise in artificial cinematic prophecy. We are made to know what is coming next. Suddenly the phone ... ... [click] "Hello?"

Door bursts, axe falls, blood spills, and the shine on the shoe is sharp as a blade. Everything happens as if in reverse. Time is out of joint.

Nothing can be a hard thing to know.

Blackness, blankness, no memory, until she awoke attached to a drip in the hospital bed. The drugs she takes she doesn't know what they do or why they are prescribed. They are prescribed to keep her from going mad. She goes mad all the time.

Dear Glenda and Paul Paul and Glenda my dears this is a new typewriter so everything's gonna be misspelled a new typewriter to begin the new story because...

I am not going to be able to see you in France but then you are not going to be able to see me in France...the former because...

I HAVE FALLEN IN LOVE!!!! I finally found the exclamation marks!!!! and there he is!!! back in an hour....

the night is falling.

.

.

Well a week later: I AM GETTING LAZY (what a relief!) I mean no more endless workworkwork I really am lazy writing all the time histories no stories about New York everything's pouring out of me. And I have no desire to speak to anyone here, I don't quite no why, all of me has gone into retreat except for letters. I drink wine and write. And redreadredread a Georges Sand kick: what a wonderful woman she was! Did what she wanted, an aristocrat, the true kind, of manners: meaning complexity no t just mememememem, like Henry James able to portray (here is real entertainment, madame) women. PORTRAIT OF A? THE? DOVE. Now beginning to relax, waters always lapping in my ear, cold here in Seattle, because always damp, not much else, anarchists at the corners of perception like a Conrad story, grey and bricks, oh the phone rang. Pland are to stay here for a year, for there is no one to talk to, except Logie, and the bleakness cannot last lifelong, then onto Paris and get a house there (outside Paris) or in England, for by then all of my grandmother's money will have come through (it is UNbelievable, but it takes two years for money to come through a will, well the lawyers will probably have it all) but we are still leaving the USA you can't imagine how wierd it is here now no more "soft fascism" but mind control depression will get wierder, the fear disallows people thinking they have even the most minimal control over their lives for revolt much less pride. Anarchists lurk out of perception... I've been going through many changes in relation to Logie (the guy I'm living with) this is the first time I've ever lived with a guy (beyond teenagehood and obsessions with mom and dad) where I've done more than consider what the guy can do for me (prostitution); I mean, for the first time in my life I have to consider being a woman and not just a man in a God-or-Fate-Being-Inconsiderate drag. It is rough but I feel good and the writing isn't stopping. At the same time, especially Glenda reading this incredibl e book GYN/ECOLOGY by Mary Daly, a bit programmatic meaning boring meaning concerned with moralistic meaning but this best part AND THE MOST EXCITING I'VE EVER SEEN a doing of langauage re with twined spinning femininity. Daphne Marlatt who is a very dear friend and a GOOD WRITER and getting GUTSIER up in Vancouver who will write you I hope because I tell everyone about you put me on to this. Books mean so much more now I'm out of NYC and don't hsave fashion weighing on me and can FEEL. Meme what I can feel. No what people want me. I think fame is the most horrible soul-wrecking thing there is.
So soon I shall be, for what is a year? living within range of you and we shall TALK: not these endless letters. I haven't been able to do business for you because of the move and all of my NYC friends except for Diego who understands are upset with me especially boyfriends such as Jeffrey and I am not getting royalties etc. But except for the this snivelling shit the publishing is not blown and I will have bigger possibilities in a month tl there is a press here and I just have to find my space enought o start working things out. I wish I could see you soon, but as love is very important, I do this and don't be angry, but keep in touch: I love you both. What else? Just books: am reading Benjamin, Steinbeck - such snobbery in this country even among poets, NYC controls taste even UNDERGROUND taste so Steinbeck is NOT EXPERIMENTAL NO GOOD he is incredible no more room or so much all my love Kathy- 111 Bell St. Seattle, Wash. 98121 206-682-7535

The night is falling

To watch the gutsy woman walk into the room, walk into Paris, dressed as Binoche, dressed as Kathy. To be strong and desirous to kick around the perfumed egos. To be lazy and to be strong. To be deep, to be intense, to seek, but not to seek fame. Where is fashion? Out in the harbour. To keep aspirations at the forefront of the mind. To reshape the mind, to find fresh determination.

To find love. To have love! To exclaim one's love!!! To lift me off my feet!!!

Is one to write and hold back the blows? Is one to go forward, to unleash the passion within? I AM PASSION. I am not about *vast, cold, commodious, respectable rooms, through whose window-panes one sees a snow-covered landscape, and across whose acres of sober-hued carpet one looks in vain for a fireplace, or a fire.* I AM THAT FIRE. I AM EXPENDITURE. I AM LOSING MYSELF. I AM NOT DELICACY.

I LOVE REDDING. I LOVE READING. I read as much as my wretched stomach will allow. I never give up on it. I will never refrain from reading. Age does not impede the process. But one can mingle in the world with fresh perceptions only when one is young. The great thing is to be saturated with something—that is, in one way or another, with life. I chose the form of my saturation. I spend only the interest of my capital.

Every passion borders on the chaotic, but the collector's passion borders on the chaos of memories. A collection is a disorder to which habit has accommodated itself to such a degree that it can become an order. There might be a dread to collecting, but there is no dread to reading, only a dread to not being able to re-read. A fear of re-dreading. There is no room and yet so much. There is no city and yet the filling of the emptiness outside. There is a crowd, but there are no people. There is only love to fill myself with.

And love needs no language. I am lazy when I'm in love. I read but I do not write. I read and I fuck. I fuck and I keep fucking. I do not need to read about love, only to live it. I can read about sex and still live it. There is no limit to the language of fucking. It is there on the page and we are drawn to it, we have an inner magnet to draw us to it. Our passions burst through the walls of language, as if the language is itself repressed, and wishes to be penetrated into its inner being.

O. If it wasn't the story. I want a history, not another story. Not to spread myself to get fucked but to get love. Men don't understand. I refuse to let my body become my father's desire.

RESOURCES

Intimate Journals: Charles Baudelaire (trans Christopher Isherwood)
Les Enfants du Siècle: Diane Kurys
Theory of Fiction: Henry James
Illuminations: Walter Benjamin (trans Harry Zohn)
Minima Moralia: Theodor Adorno (trans E.F.N.Jephcott)
Great Expectations: Kathy Acker

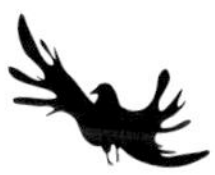

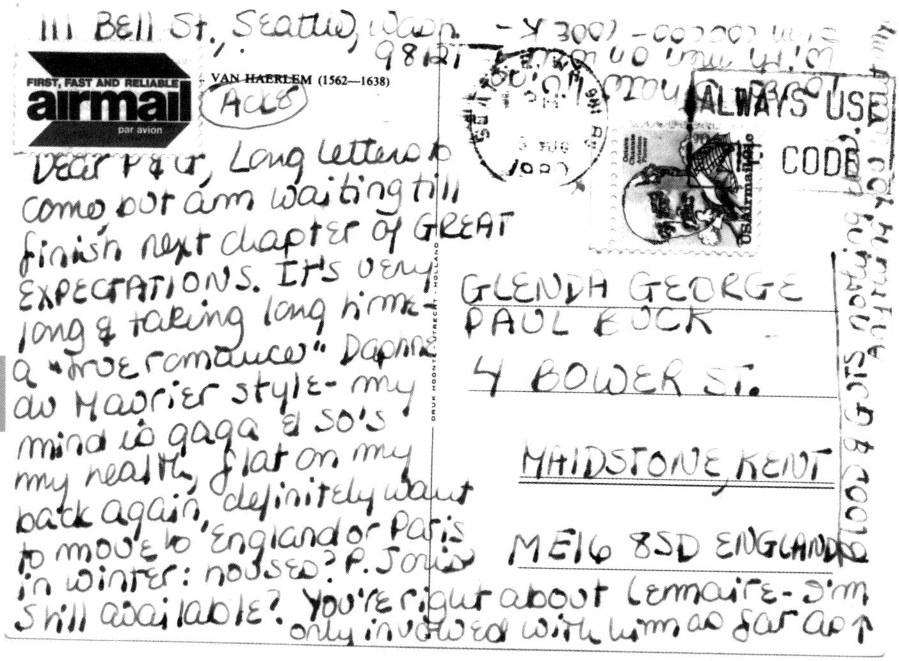
111 Bell St., Seattle, Wash. 98121

FIRST, FAST AND RELIABLE airmail par avion

VAN HAERLEM (1562—1638)

ALWAYS USE ZIP CODE

Dear P & G, Long letter to come but am waiting till finish next chapter of GREAT EXPECTATIONS. It's very long & taking long time - a "true romance" Daphne du Maurier style - my mind is gaga & so's my health, flat on my back again, definitely want to move to England or Paris in winter: housed? P. Jones still available? You're right about Lemaire - I'm only involved with him as far as ↑

GLENDA GEORGE
PAUL BUCK
4 BOWER ST.
MAIDSTONE, KENT
ME16 8SD ENGLAND

My cunt used to be a men's toilet. Or should I say: My cunt used to be a gents' toilet. Cos I had every intention of setting Daphne du Maurier as my stylist. And you know, style rules. Like George, you gotta have style.

So, we start the fiction. We start the writing. Dear dreams, Dear Mommie Dearest,

You are the only thing that matters. You are my hope and I live for and in you. You are rawness and wildness, the colours, the scents, passion, events appearing. You are things I live for. Please take me over.

If I write you into the story do you exist?

Demands for communication are both presumptuous and irrelevant. The observer usually will see what his fears and hopes and learning teach him to see. But if he can escape these demands that hold up a mirror to himself, then perhaps some of the implications of the work may be felt. But whatever is seen or felt it should be remembered that for me these paintings had to be something else. It is the price one has to pay for clarity when one's means are honoured only as an instrument of seduction or assault.

There are very few real references in the work, and the references are not to popular culture or to art, but perhaps to artlike things. Look, I think there's confusion between an image that comes from somewhere and a reference. I don't think of things as references unless they really refer to something else.

There's no narrative. There really is none, there isn't one.

There's no story?

Right. None at all.

You see, my way of thinking keys into your notion of the autonomy of the work, its abstractness.

I think about a couple of different things that appear, that have lived their lives in the arena of popular culture, but I don't think of them as popular. One is a comedy, and the other is pornography. Those are two things that are important to me for themselves. Not as a comment on the society that produces them, but in their own mechanistic ways, you know, in a detached way.

Dreams by themselves aren't enough to destroy the blanket of dullness.

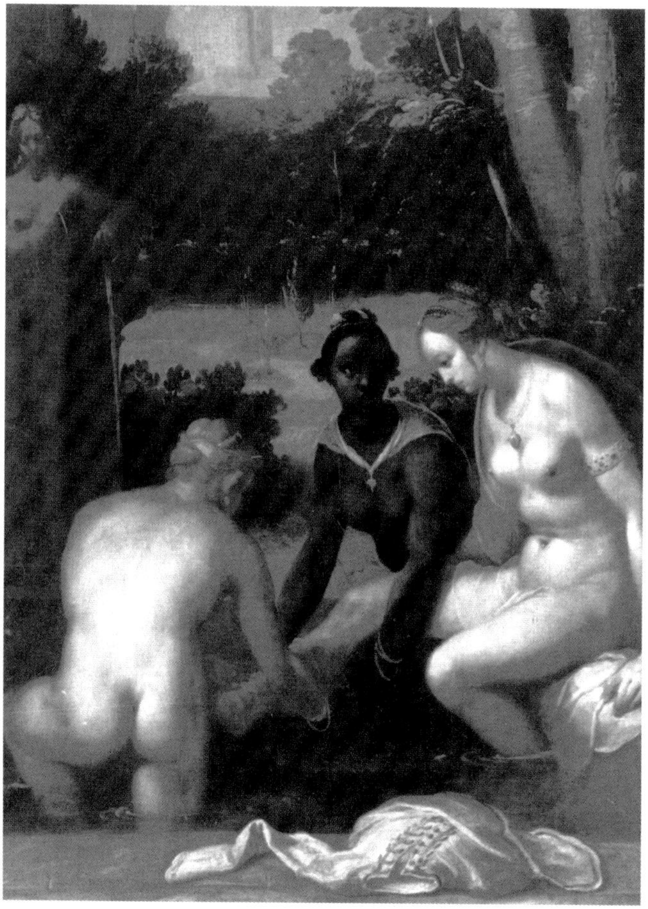

You notice I'm writing in code.

AND MY PRINCIPLE STANDS: EACH BOOK GLEAMS AT US FROM ITS SHELF, EACH IN ITS OWN FIERCE INDIVIDUALITY, EACH TO BE RECKONED WITH.

It's hard to get beyond mommie:

My legs are spread wide. Knees up. Fish open. One hand on clit.

Left leg raised up. Right leg bent and horizontal. Hand under left leg. Middle finger all way in cunt.

Legs spread, arse up. Third and fourth fingers, V open cunt wide.

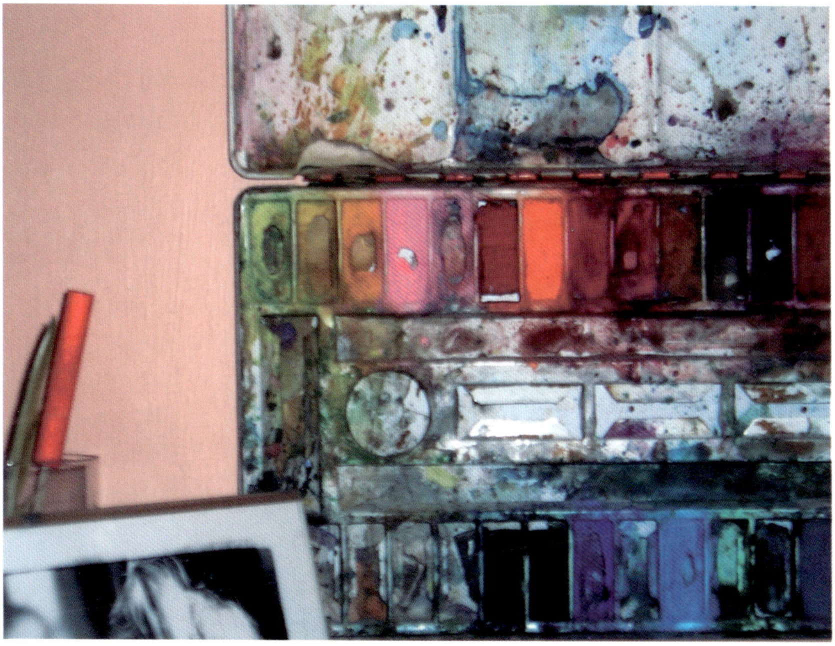

RESOURCES

Great Expectations: Kathy Acker

Blood and Guts in High School: Kathy Acker

Clyfford Still in 15 Americans

David Salle interviewed by Robert Pincus-Witten

The Scorpions: Robert Kelly

Dear Paul,

I've been travelling in California - actually after seeing as many San Franciscan poets as could fit into three days, sat on a beach in Southern California for weeks - after a severe illness, and just returned last night, so am answering your letter probably much too late, for which I am sorry, but... Of course I don't give magazines in the same country the same material; I do my best to keep everything straight. If I have made a mistake, please tell me. I could have made a mistake, because when I moved from New York to here, someone stole about everything, in dfact I didn't even have a typewriter until two weeks ago, and all my accounts of what I sent where were lost. I told Hodgkiss (is that his name?) to publish the first chapter of GREAT EXPECTATIONS. I hope there's no overlap; I simply don't remember what you planned to publish in CURTAINS and it was long ago. I repeat again, because I don't want to mess up our friendship, I am usually very careful about this sort of thing, and I hope there's no overlap. As for my publishing in English magazines generally as long as there's no overlap: I do think it's O/K/ for my work to get that sort of distribution; you don't feel if you publish me in CURTAINS, I shouldn't allow any other English magazine to publish me? Of course I'd rather publish in CURTAINS than any other mag. As for the IT piece, that was set back in Amsterdam at the time we met.

Since I haven't had access to a typewriter I haven't been able to type up next, actually five, chapters of GREAT EXPECTATIONS, and plan to do so now, to shut myself up in this room for a month, until I have to go to San Francisco in November and December to teach a course on performance!!!! at the Art Institute and then... I don't know. Seattle is bleak and horrible and I believe I'm too old and rotty to live with anyone. All I need to do is write anyway that's the only thing

The men who are part of my life aren't really part of my life. How can I give up my desires? That is what men want. I can't do that. I think I will never live with a man again, never marry again. I need total affection, desperately, but do I need to go as far as to write a will so that HE automatically shares my wealth, whatever that wealth will be. I can un-make that will, if all fails. I can un-make my texts when I fail. I FAIL ALL THE TIME. That is the *pleasure* of my life. TO FAIL. Is this thing I call desire really a desire to fail? Is there any desire for happiness? Do I just crave affection, desperately? I am a scared little shit. I know that. I am nothing. I always knew that.

How to live with desire? How to desire by burying desire? How to indulge in desire by not desiring indulgence? Desire is the Master. And desire is to be hated. Oh Lord. Oh oh

I can cast my texts into the fire. I can leave them behind, ask others to pack for me, treat them badly so they get lost. I can instruct people to destroy them, to tell them never to publish them, and yet know that ultimately they will be published, that someone will disregard copyright, or watch time slip away from time, let the timelessness of the text rule. Once written who can stop their inevitable fate? Should anyone stop their endless spiral into publication?

I don't live on a desert island. I used to think I did, just for a moment, one mad moment of aberration. In the beginning the world was beautiful. On that desert island. Now all is shit. Discuss.

Well, class. Discuss. I'm your new teacher.

I am not your slave, I am your whore. That is what a teacher should be.

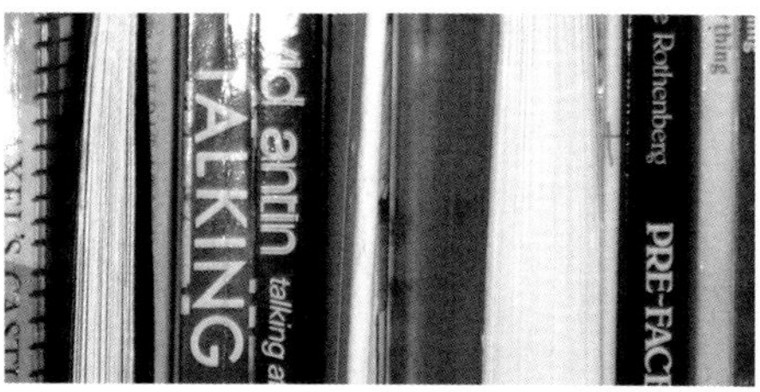

I am living in a book. I am floating on water, I am propped against a bar. I am everywhere. I am god, or like god. Because most places are godforsaken holes. And I don't know where I want to go with that vertiginous phrase, those words that spin into a black hole for me. Through which I drop. That void in which I am to write. Trying to escape. I live on an island. Not a desert island. That can be boring. That only allows me to drag my trunk around, across the sands. I like lying on the sand, and and and I would like the island a whole lot better if it had books, if it is a library. I live in a library. That is where my desire is. IS. Is *situated*. Do I want

I can do halfway decently and... oh oh oh. America is so bleak and horrible and endless away from the decaying urban centers. Claustrophobia the worst. I'm losing laughing here na d read Daphne du Maurier and endless crummy romantic reading wgich is real unrecognized women's genre and strong pro-marriage etc. (slvery?) propaganda, the worst is the bleakness: three walls in my mind and I get sick. Don't know what I'll do after teaching gig ends, probably head East; have to settle down to finish novel. Stonehill seemed about to do BLLOOD AND GUTS and is now fucking up again but they registered it with the IRS as a tax loss for this year so I'm going to blackmail them as far as possible into getting that damn book out cause it's been too long and being book-constipated is the worst constipation in the world. Otherwise evrything goes well. I just hate being oin the outlands so much: I feel cut off from everythingone. Read new Greene Capote now on Russian formalists post-Revolution saw two beautiful Russian Constructivists shows. Malevich is the best candy going. Pure inspiration. The Kipper Kids are on TV now! (I teach after them in SF/) Will ask around about HONEYMOON KILLERS publishing - oh the Kippers are just wonderful I don't care if they are arty what will I do after them I don't know how to do anything I am totally incapable. Why the hell are these people hiring me? J effrey Goldberg just wrote he losyt your address and what is it he'll send you a NYMPHO immediately. He's a total fuck-up. Like my friend Elly Antin I'm pissed at the world. Sob sob sob. Anywhere but here. How to get from boring women's problems to Baudelaire. How who cares about high culture.

Dear Glenda my dear, I shall write you a separate letter.

Now I am well....... here comes The AVENGERS////

LOVELOVELOVE THE K

books to escape love? To escape affection? Are the books my affection? Do they love me as much as I love and desire them? Love IS. *Situated.* I roll through the shelves. I am a boat rolling along the shelves, in a library, yes, a library, not a bookshop. Cos in a library I can take down those books and read them for as long as I like. Commerce is no part of the exchange. I do not have to pay to read. I do not have to own them. I do not own these texts, as I do not own my texts. I write them, but they come from elsewhere. I change them, I have pleasure with them. I desire them and love them. I pleasure them. They appear as other texts. But am I to keep those texts close to my chest, are they to stay in my belly? Do they go into the world sideways or full on, it doesn't matter which way? Have their own lives, to fight the sharks, to struggle with whatever I chose to talk about in those texts. If I say I LOVE someone is that important? If I say I hate someone, that they are a total shit, is that important? Why should they get upset? They probably think I AM A TOTAL SCAREDY SHIT. WHICH I AM, JUST AS MUCH AS I THINK THEY ARE TOTAL SHIT. So what? DON'T GET YOUR LITTLE EGOS IN A TWIST. DON'T THINK YOU ARE MORE IMPORTANT THAN YOU ARE. LOOK IN THE MIRROR.

RIPS IN THE MIRROR. Can't you see?

What do you expect from the looking glass? Do you wish to see cracks, a multi-faceted play, an author who multiplies in a Pessoan manner, or the expanding and contracting, living and breeeathing, chest of the stern(e) one? Am I these? Or must I extend you. & them. & me. & Men. Is the need to reveal devices important? Do I want a perpetual present, or presence, rather than a time travel? Is timelessness the nature of writing itself?

Gerty Stein says that she likes to look at the picture part of it (meaning, modern art), and that the other parts interest her much less. That is followed by another who writes that he is interested in the yellow in de Kooning. Then pink. Then grey. "The chance to stare at these painted colours, not works of art or experiences of form, and certainly not the various figurative pretexts, although the remnants of the faces of women are certainly unavoidable."

I skid across the text, taking fragments that appeal to me. Is that it? Is that all there is?, Peggy sings before the avenging Peel comes to the rescue. Particularly when she becomes the Queen of Sin in the Hellfire Club, spiked collar and black corset, as if eyes directed towards a Corman Poe. Not that the States saw it, trimmed for UK, banned in US.

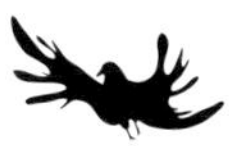

RESOURCES

Great Expectations: Kathy Acker
Blood and Guts in High School: Kathy Acker
The Prison-House of Language: Frederic Jameson
Towards a Libidinal Economy of Three Modern Painters: Frederic Jameson

PSYCHIC BROTHEL

Marc meets his drunken friend Carlo by the fountain in the piazza. Carlo was supposed to be playing piano tonight at the Psychic Brothel, a jazz bar in New Hackney. "Look at this fucking place. A cosmetic yuppie dream of urban authenticity: Canal side Industrial Picturesque. I've seen it before so many times. You can always tell it's happening when the cafes fill up with white pregnant middle-class 30 something mothers and gay clones singing the praises of *Beyoncé*. I met a guy once in the toilets of a public bathhouse in Slovenia. An Italian guy. He was desperate. I'd just finished sucking him off. He was shaking like a wreck. I asked him what was wrong. He said he was terrified of being killed by a terrorist bomb. That's why he pretty much lived in the toilet. "All those people", he said, "packed so tightly together. I don't want to die like that!" I didn't know this guy but felt the need to console him for some reason. "Accidents will happen", I told him. "They've got to happen to someone. Terrorist action will happen. Someone has got to be blown up...Most importantly don't consider every action as a potential death trap the moment before you take it, unless you really do want to drive yourself into a death vortex".

Carlo hurls bottle against the canal wall and stumbles into the road.
Marc catches him before he falls.

"Listen Marco, fast-fading pianists like you asslick the Process like you asslick everything that will help your 'profile'. You'll exploit anything you can get your hands on. This is a Middle class Kill City project – It's all rich/poor, the entire planet. Total Ghettofication is everywhere. Each and everyone of us here are at each and every fucking moment a living breathing instance of gentrification/ghettofication and therefore deserve everything we get. That German psychic is no different. What would you rather be Marco, an evolved Health Food-eating Eco-Consciousness with an ISA and a fair-trade mortgage or a Shit-eating Black Savage with a machete and a sack of crack?"

"Carlo, can't you drop that Thomas Stuart Prophet shit! I'm sick of hearing it. And what good is it doing you or anyone else. Neither time nor space actually expand, they merely alter relations by formal stages. We are those changes and relations, contracting, individuating, etc...but the mind space of the new city is severely difficult to map in any traditional way. There is just moving and there are different ways of moving. Or: there is moving all over at the same time and there is moving linearly. If everything is moving-all-over-the-place-no-time, anything is everything. If this is so, how can I differentiate? How can there be stories? Consciousness just is: no time. But any emotion presupposes differentiation. Differentiation presumes time, at least BEFORE and NOW. A narrative is an emotional moving. It is already producing after-effects before any words have been discussed... No one is sure how to get into it anymore, where anyone is, what is going on, if they've

Sorry for the silence - I've been working, serving drinks and serving time. So much noise and chatter left me nothing to say to you, used me up for anything better. At the end of the day I was spent, loose like change. Walking home I'd number my steps and it was like counting back with a hypnotist - you are feeling calm, you are feeling sleepy. There! - I'm gone!

Today I'm back sitting quietly with the artist.

A different pose - lying on my right side, legs crossed (good girl), elbow propped beneath me, my right hand free to spread across the pages of the notebook in which I speak. My left hand is in my lap. My mind moves toward you.

Desire and experience are good teachers, but you're no whore, my Kathy! On that island with your unpredictable father you're more like Miranda. Curious, open, spread wide to knowledge like a sunflower to the sun, naked like me.

We shared a few words this evening, the artist and I, over cups of black coffee with brandy in it, as I lay there. He said some things that made me think. "The naked," he said "are much more direct. The naked possess the power to signify."

"It is entirely possible without words

got the gist, is it really happening [we are born, WE ARE DEAD, we emerge/emerse the mother] leaving a crypto-psychism of our knowledge which, earth-loop and ghost-like, lives on, adumbrating our fatalities whereby our past constantly re-enters us. Like Hari's resurrection from Solaris- a kind orgasm re-entering, phantasm hysteria porno".

Carlo thinks Marco is an intellectual snob and total fucking div.

"Look, Marco, I am the proletarian of the piano-forte and you are the bourgeoisie. You play for art and enjoy it and I play for a living. It's not the same thing. Body-based process writing? I want it like fresh pulsings from the base up. I want it like revolution. I want it like I want my cock sucked. For me the piano is like the body of a beautiful woman. And I tickle her...like a mate of the Black Tarantula...then BAM! her fangs are in my neck and she's sucking the life out of me".

Suddenly they hear a scream from the canal path. "Perhaps that's another one getting murdered. I drink to you! Deflowered virgin!" Carlo shouts.

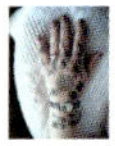

Marc thinks Carlo is a total fucking nihilist.

Time unfolds determinations, but nothing really happens, exactly as it is possible to calculate all the positions of the pendulum from its initial position without the actual fall of the pendulum adding any new information. The same is true of this rotting text...(rotting being produced granularity) if development is understood as the unfolding of potentialities, a problem, as is well known, that Piaget tackled twice in the growth of molluscs and of child intelligence. (?)

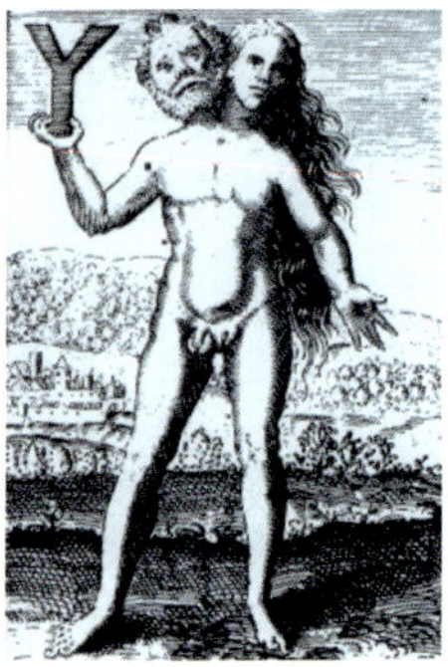

Marc is telling the police officers what he saw when he came into the victims apartment. There were deranged paintings lining the wall.

One of them seems to be missing.

to make oneself clear." I replied. "It is entirely possible without clothes to make oneself clear."

"Yes," he said. "But there's something between me and your nakedness, between the artist and the model. You are not clear. Nothing is transparent. You are veiled in flesh and in silence, and they sit between us like the shadow and the ghost. Before that ghost the artist cries out in terror."

He paused.

"But he must persist," he resumed. "I am *urged* by you, by your silence, by your eyes, and your body, to continue. I have to get beyond what the looking-glass shows - down into the rabbit-hole depth of you."

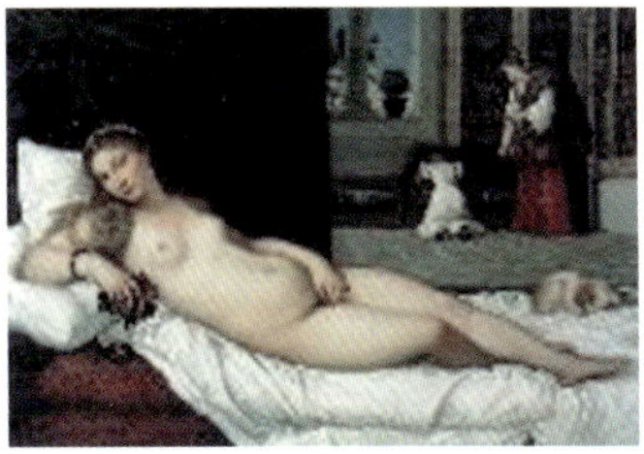

Beyond the surface - beneath clothes, passing facial expressions, transitory thoughts, my ideas about who I am. Way below the things I'd list as being my essence down to that spark which illuminates every one of us. This isn't about 'the picture part', exercises in pattern and colour. Leave that to others, those who apologise that the remnants of women's faces are unavoidable. Those tone poems, those songs to colour, are theirs. But they are songs only of the mind, that part that delights in dissection.

"Have you changed anything? he asks the police officer.

"Are you crazy?"

"No, I just had an impression. There were some crude figures on a stage. Some crazy writing. It's probably nothing".

"What were you doing at the time of the murder?"

"I was in the waiting room of the museum library. A teenage girl with red-hair was sitting next to me. She asked me what I was researching. "I'm doing some stuff on The Name of the Father and The Mother's Law," I tell her. "Oh really", she says, "That's great. So you're just researching your family then. I didn't know you could do that sort of thing here". But there was something else. What was it?

[Whether it...recovering remembrance...where to begin...the choice will determine the development of the story...so it's the initial choice that becomes imperative...I probably made a mistake already by telling him this...should have gone straight into the gallery...but which picture.... the last one I remember?...the most memorable?...] There was a green picture composed directly onto the wall of the gallery, a collage in a room full of works painted directly on to the wall.... I was going to have to give a talk about something...couldn't remember what...two lectures to give in two days, three articles to write before next week... someone complimented me on giving a lecture at such a prestigious institution...what lecture? Something about Women in Art and Popular Culture, tomorrow, in the main gallery. So I had to get on with that...but that day I had to give a lecture to my students. I thought maybe I could use that time to develop the lecture...but I was supposed to be talking about something else. What was it? I couldn't remember. So I'll talk about the difficulty of remembering things when your spread too wide on the margins of artworld".

" Maybe you don't understand the importance of what you saw. Sometimes what you see and what you imagine get mixed up in your memory like a cocktail".

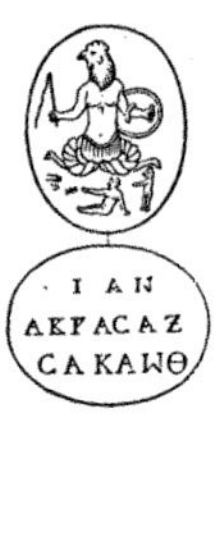

He affirms a different non-existence. He sings the body electric – elemental – past all that me, a something among somethings, down to where I am when I am nobody. It's tough enough to do it to yourself, but the artist has to do it at a distance, too. And how careful he must be to go beyond his own looking-glass world as well as mine; it is terrible, it is frightening (ego-fear, that child within us that clings, clings, clings to consciousness) to walk naked along that absent way.

Come: let's get away from it all.

Daphne

545 Ashbury #1
SF, CA 94117

23 Sept 80

Dear Kathy,

Doubt if you'd remember me (I gave you a copy of my STRETCHING THE AGAPE BRA book at 80 Langton St when you were in town). Anyway I was wondering if you might have something to contribute to next issue of SOUP magazine which will focus on New Narrative writing. Bruce Boone has a long essay (critically brilliant I think) on language poets (taking off from TALKS issue of HILLS specifically) & there will be work from writers of color as well as (possibily, they've been asked anyway) a few writers better known nationally (ie: Paul Bowles, Denise Levertov, Phil Whalen). Deadline for next issue is Oct. 31.

Enclosed is 1st issue of SOUP. Had been meaning to send this to you anyway as Anne Waldman has a piece in it dedicated to you. Hoping to hear from you soon.

Best,

Steve Abbott

Steve Abbott

also some new prose poem

Dear Paul & Glenda - Want to write you both long long letters, but (meanwhile) here I am at Post Office - with only today's mail as paper - to send a manuscript to ART FORUM - and want you to see these new chapters of GREAT EXPECTATIONS (which are about a third of the new section, I'm typing slowly cause I owe various people various essays including the 5th International Congress of Psychoanalysis, whatever that is, hee hee). I plan to go to England as soon as I stick my stuff at least somewhere semi-permanently in this damn country which is blowing up with Reagan's head as a fuse anyway cause I can't keep lugging 3000 books around I ain't Atlas & books aren't as interesting as worlds or are they or are they worlds? Meanwhile, my mind, where has language gone to the love relation here is Seattle has gone blotto - the kid is still totally charming so it's all painful, but it's like having a baby, & I'm not even stable enough to be one & I can't afford someone less stable than me - I guess I can't afford to fuck & I love to FUCK SOB SOB SOB no more ROOM

Will write & send my new NYMPHO, ME

LOVE

SOB SOB SOB. There ain't mush room in London either. One big room that people keep shoving chairs into. Ionesco's been there before. Before that door we still keep shoving them in. They are called artists. They pour from the art schools and think they'll make it as artists. Or actually they don't really delude themselves. They just don't think about it. Well it's not the arts schools fault. They gotta eat. They gotta fund artists who can't earn money from art but only from teaching. Loop the loop. So out they pop from between the spread wide legs of art education. Be an artist. Nothing else to do. As they can't actually produce art, they spend their time, which they have loads of, fucking each other, running through the permutations, though with no sense of maths or logic, they do art nothing else, it's total chaos and random and thus the chances of hitting it right, scoring and winning the lottery, becoming famous or even becoming a famous artist are reduced. Best to go straight to the gallery and fuck the brains out of the owner, gender irrelevant. Bugger their politics. Bugger all politics of the art system. Commodity purchasing is commodity purchasing. Ethics and morality have minimal roles to play. Still end up same way.

RESOURCES
Great Expectations: Kathy Acker

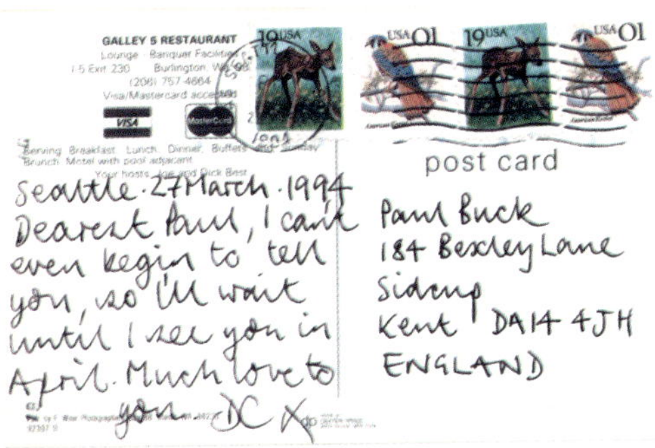
GALLEY 5 RESTAURANT
post card
Seattle · 27 March · 1994
Dearest Paul, I can't even begin to tell you, so I'll wait until I see you in April. Much love to you. DC x
Paul Buck
184 Bexley Lane
Sidcup
Kent DA14 4JH
ENGLAND

David Coulter

Dear Paul,

Just wrote Glenda and in letter put some pertinent info like forwarding addresses future plans so can she give you info so I don't have to repeat? I AM being tacky. I'm SO glad you like GREAT EXPECTATIONS and maybe it's tacky of me but HAITI is also my least favorite, it was just one thing, not a complex painting, and besides its YOU yours is the first feedback I've recieved ion the new stuff and of course endless worries: you don't know what you're doing anymore kid you're off on your own process track no one will ever understand you're using language not language but given language, as in Flaubert's, like paint, now just given material, sculpting it, who the fuck does that? They're all concerned with meaning. Language has to MEAN if there's a storyline we've ALL got a world-view isn't that why we write, we're not playing being devious, questioning escaping, all the things psychos do, you're right, Paul, you, me, Glenda the French writers- otherwise the work is so misunderstood. When people now say I want to tell what I thought off....of... I know what's coming and say SHUT UP cause I'm so sick of hearing WHY ARE YOU SO VIOLENT? ARE YOU A SEX MANIAC? WHEN CAN I FUCK YOU? I'll send you a copy of FLORIDA with copy of essay I just wrote for some Italian psychoanalytic mag - why they wanted something me not know maybe they think I'm a sex-psycho case too. Speaking of sex-psychos I'm treasuring HONEYMOON until I can savor it in SF (three more weeks to go! cause here everything is so desperate and violence I just keep working working putting out to keep from feeling. I've been finally talking to people around here, trying to get as realistic (am I being 19th c.?) a picture of the guy I've been living with my reactions to him, and my feeling is -cliche: he has deep-rooted problems. Well, I can't

WHY ARE YOU SO VIOLENT? ARE YOU A SEX MANIAC? WHEN CAN I FUCK YOU? In other words the usual. A case of red and more red, and reading, and more reading. And then to set to work, brush in hand.

First the red. Do you remember those red chairs, high-backed, in that restaurant off Boulevard St Germain where we ate? Alice terrain, except Jean Paris was more real than anything Lewis could have produced. Did we go into that café round the corner that night, the one I always frequented with Manchette? No, I don't think so. Red, that car we pissed against. I say we, I'm being generous. Everything was always red, always well & truly read. How one can find words within words in one language that can drive a text off along a different boulevard, driving without a car. Whether she was in it. Was she? I saw her in here. Right from the start. The here is Now. Is IS. We live in this presence, this movement across the page, along the line, and down.

Another frame. Another page.

Nothing can come of nothing, whereas, of course, everything comes from nothing.

As it is extremely hard to define red in positive terms, I shall therefore do it in negative. Red then is not red. And here I must object to a third error concerning it, which is, that it is in no place; which is an indirect way of depriving it of its existence; whereas indeed it possesses the greatest and noblest place on this earth, viz. redness. But indeed this mistake had been sufficiently refuted by many very wise men; who, having spent their whole lives in contemplation and pursuit of red, have at last gravely concluded—that there is red in this world.

Farther, as red is not red, so everything which is not red is red; and wherever red is not red is: a very large allowance in its favour, as must appear to persons well skilled in human affairs.

This is a secret not known to all readers, and want of this knowledge hath occasioned much puzzling; for where a book or chapter or paragraph hath seemed to the reader to contain red, his modesty hath sometimes persuaded him that the true meaning of the author hath escaped him, instead

do anything more, we got quite to the edge, so it's just a matter of marking time, out I go, I'll be human again. Just got a new collection of Foucault's essays, he talks in first essay about sex always being about that limit, over-the-limit, god knows yes. But there has to be preservation enough, at least for me, to write. And read HONEYMOON. I did read VIOLATIONS which is incredible: the language in its non-givingness as far as prettiness that easiness throws me back to the point, not a point of course but more than intention:concern. What is of importance. Not: this is how things are, but: in the meananderings (language) the statements so denotatively precise they can't mean anything else and so almost bracket themselves (a little like Blanchot's style) are not philosophical but are themselves. Not madness (I'm thinking here of som some essay I just read I forget whose, where he I think it's a he, says how limited madness is, restrained by normalcy, where we want are something else. The intro to the Foucault essays?) I'm mean just what is and at that this point no duality between kanguage and (like kangaroos) language and what it's a story of. A different kind of story than ELMER, and actual BEING_HERE. HERE HERE HERE HERE. (Don't refer to because of course her is included).

TIGHT AS LEGS sounds good. How about I send FLORIDA and essay in this eletter, page in next letter? I'll be in SF then. Oh my dear IT'S SO GOOD TO HEAR FROM YOU!!!! Love,K

of concluding, as in reality the fact was, that the author in the said book, etc., did truly and bona fide mean red.

In fact, this mistake arises from a too vulgar error among persons unacquainted with the mystery of writing, who imagine it impossible that a man should sit down to write without any meaning at all! whereas, in reality, red is more common: for, not to instance in myself, who had confessedly set down to write this essay with red in my head, or, which is much the same thing, to write about red, it may be incontestably proved, *ab effectu*, that red is commoner among the moderns.

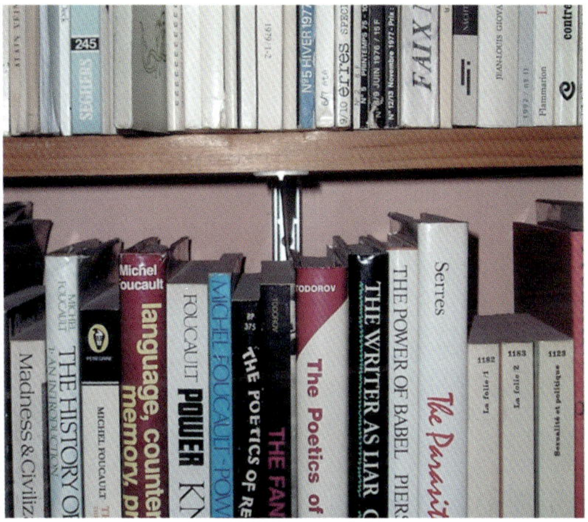

We have not in the least liberated sexuality, though we have, to be exact, carried it to its limits: the limit of consciousness, because it ultimately dictates the only possible reading of our unconscious; the limit of the law, since it seems the sole substance of universal taboos; the limit of language, since it traces that line of foam showing just how far speech may advance upon the sands of silence. Thus, it is not through sexuality that we communicate with the orderly and pleasingly profane world of animals; rather, sexuality is a fissure—not one which surrounded us as the basis of our isolation or individuality, but one which marks the limit within us and designates us as a limit.

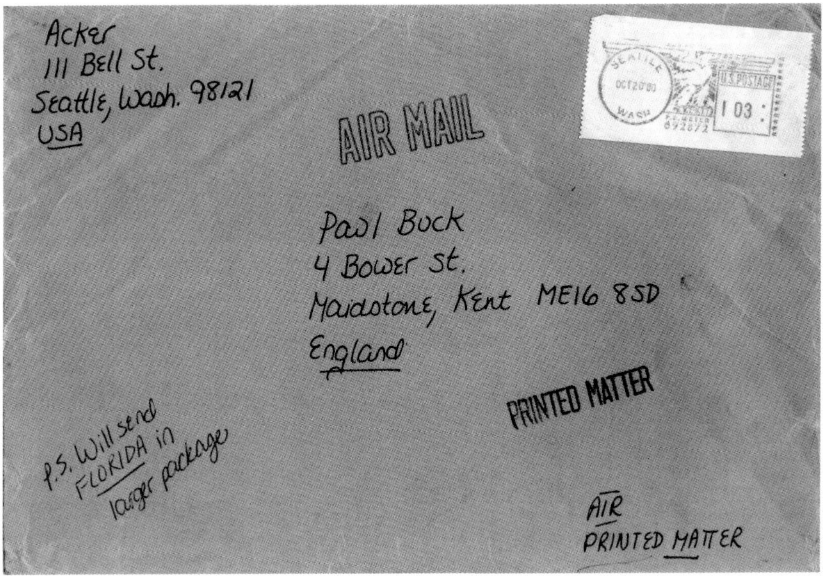
Acker
111 Bell St.
Seattle, Wash. 98121
USA
AIR MAIL
SEATTLE WASH
OCT 20 '80
U.S. POSTAGE
1 03
692872
Paul Buck
4 Bower St.
Maidstone, Kent ME16 8SD
England
PRINTED MATTER
P.S. Will send FLORIDA in larger package
AIR
PRINTED MATTER

What I call night differs from the darkness of thoughts: night possesses the violence of light. Yes, night: the youth and the intoxication of thinking.

[Will you come out of the night?

[I tried masturbating. I tried.

Scene. A place of redness. Velvet curtains.

I know the extraordinary calmness one feels at the moment of performing the theft, and the fear that accompanies it.

My body is afraid.

No sooner do I get inside than I'm sure I'll come out with a jewel. A ring or handcuffs.

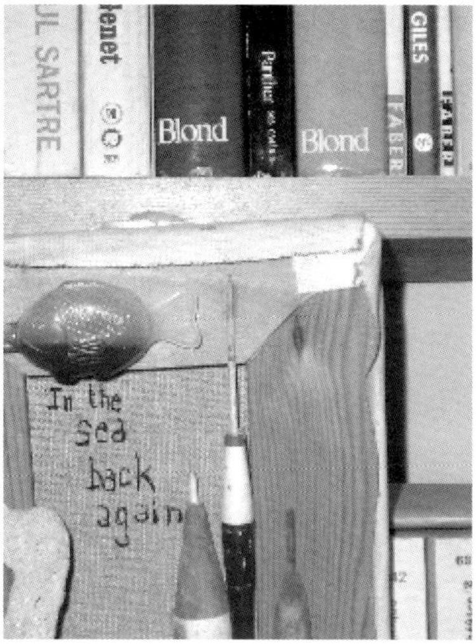

My cells seem to be transmitting to one another a wave, an undulating movement, which is the very substance of calm. I am alive with thought from my heels to the back of my neck. I accompany the wave. It is born of fear. Without it there would not be this calm in which my body bathes—which my body attains.

For a half hour I shall be operating, if I am alone, in a world which is the reverse of the customary world. My heart beats loudly. My hand never trembles. Fear does not leave me for a single second. I do not think specifically of the proprietor of the place, but all my gestures evoke him in so far as they see him. I am steeped in an idea of property while I loot property.

RESOURCES

Great Expectations: Kathy Acker
An Essay on Nothing: Henry Fielding
A Preface to Transgression: Michel Foucault (trans Donald F. Bouchard & Sherry Simon)
Guilty: Georges Bataille (trans Donald F. Bouchard & Sherry Simon)
Blood and Guts in High School: Kathy Acker
The Thief's Journal: Jean Genet (trans Bernard Frechtman)

Before everything was withheld. The first sketches show a woman who, though nude, *will not let go*. Rest here, she says, be pleased with what you see. Isn't this what you wanted, to glimpse these breasts, these thighs? But turn away my gaze – I mustn't catch you peeping. Fig-leafed with coquettishness, I (me me me) was dominating and manipulating, directing his hand and your gaze. So sit me down, splay my legs, spread me wide. Let's set to work.

Apprendre à écorcher: Take up your brush and paint me, a portrait in red – red the heart, red the liver, red the lungs, red the blood, red the bowels, red the muscles, red the nerves, red the mind, red also the soul, red the artist's hand.

Once there was a young Christian, who kept his religion secret, private to himself, so as not to offend his pagan king. Thereby he gained riches and power. Over time it came to him that his wealth was nothing but a suit of gold armour, shutting out life and its pains. So he revealed himself for what he was, by publicly announcing his beliefs, and he was arrested, but this was not enough. He could barely feel anything of the tortures he was put under. He was condemned to death.

When the artist approached him he silently offered up his body. Over eight hours he was gradually dismembered – toes, fingers, feet, hands, calves, arms and legs. With each loss joy, blood and words flowed out of him in equal measure. Finally only his trunk was left. He was half alive. The last cut – they removed his head. At last, scattered in twenty-eight pieces spread wide over the bloody ground, he was exposed.

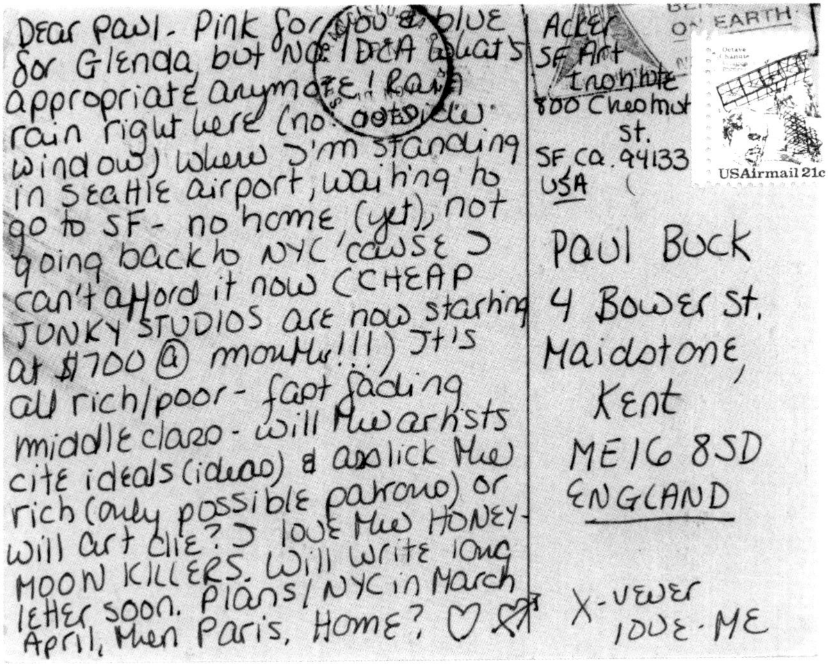

Dear Paul - Pink for you & blue
for Glenda, but NO IDEA what's
appropriate anymore! Rain
rain right here (no: outside
window) where I'm standing
in Seattle airport, waiting to
go to SF - no home (yet), not
going back to NYC 'cause I
can't afford it now (CHEAP
JUNKY STUDIOS are now starting
at $1700 @ month!!!) It's
all rich/poor - fast fading
middle class - will the artists
cite ideals (ideas) & asslick the
rich (only possible patrons) or
will art die? I love the HONEY-
MOON KILLERS. Will write long
letter soon. Plans / NYC in March
April, then Paris, Home? ♡

Acker
SF Art
Institute
800 Chestnut
St.
SF, CA. 94133
USA

Paul Buck
4 Bower St.
Maidstone,
Kent
ME16 8SD
ENGLAND

X-never
love-me

Dear and nearer further away and **blue**
for it came to be sunny in **what's**
appropriate how do they feel that **rain**
rain resumed and does it make **outside**
window)be that it should be **standing**
in being there at once once **to**
go of that one having one **not**
going is what they do have **I**
can't be a girl how can you tell **(CHEAP**
JUNKY might see how to go on **starting**
at than confusing and will be **It's**
all plainly inclined and decline **fading**
middle ones who do see me **artists**
cite mention deliberating liberatin **the**
rich have been used in that way **or**
will when let alone aimlessly **HONEY-**
MOON parts parted be stop be**long**
letter they might just as just as **March**
April does he know a great deal for**ever**
Love ME

Will literature emerge without its clothes? Meaning what? Meaning, what?

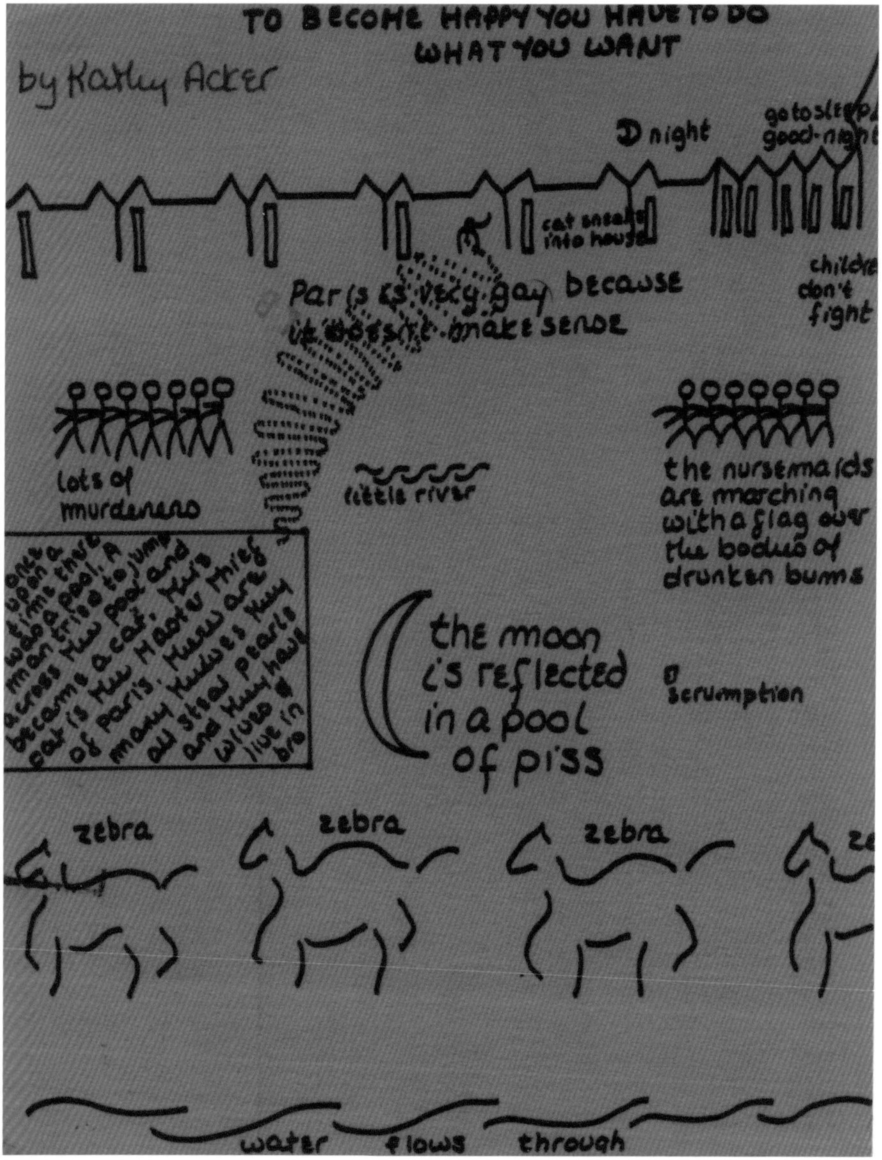

TO BECOME HAPPY YOU HAVE TO DO WHAT YOU WANT
by Kathy Acker
night
cat sneaks into house
Paris is very gay because it doesn't make sense
don't fight
lots of murderers
little river
the nursemaids are marching with a flag over the bodies of drunken bums
the moon is reflected in a pool of piss
scrumption
zebra
zebra
zebra
water flows through

The hour has come round at last, they say: literature is emerging without its clothes.

Literature used to be a hetaera. For some time she worked the streets of Antioch, trading as 'Pelagia'. After each hard night, she emerged from her house at noon, and promenaded through the city in flaunting display. Wound into a toga she wore the cloths of heaven, embroidered red and dim and dark. About her ankles, wrists, neck and brow were hung chains of gold and silver and precious stones, and with each dancing step the air was sweet with Arabian perfumes.

Who is she that goeth as a pillar of smoke of aromatical spices, of myrrh and frankincense, and of all the powders of the perfumer?

Her skin was inscribed with patterns and flourishes written in red ochre by her lovers, an amorous lexicon that was its own advertisement. As she strolled, taking her ease amongst the laurel groves, a retinue of young men and women of education and grace processed alongside, supporting a vast looking-glass in which the beauty of their mistress could be reflected to all.

RED RED RED

Behold, thou art fair, my beloved, and comely: our bed is flourishing.

A morning came when a critic saw literature's display. He was shamed by her and said "Almighty God pardon me, because the attention a courtesan has given to her adornment for one day exceeds the effort of my whole life." He berated his circle furiously, crying that the meticulous care she took in painting herself to please her earthly lovers made critics appear, by comparison, lazy.

Thou hast wounded my heart, my sister, my spouse: thou hast wounded my heart with one of thy eyes, and with one hair of thy neck.

Pelagia heard of the critic's discontent, and offered to meet with him at her home. He did not trust himself to be alone in her company, but she agreed to his condition - to sanction the presence of a number of his fellows.

The time of pruning is come: the voice of the turtle is heard in our land.

When she entered the room, she announced: "I am Literature, a sea of iniquity cresting with waves of sin; I am an abyss of perdition; I am a whirlpool, a sink to catch souls. I have misled many and deceived them." Then she sat down, and spoke with the critics.

They struck me and wounded me. They took away my veil from me.

Literature was never again seen in Antioch. But some time later, a traveller reported that during his wanderings in an antique land, he encountered a strange figure somewhere in the sands of the desert, sexless and emaciated, naked but for rough matted locks, in whose expression there still lingered traces of passion.

18 Clipper St.
SF, Ca. 94114
285-4067

Dear Paul,

Enclosed latest and last part of second tapestry in Glenda's later. letter. Oh, I can't type anymore...HOW ARE YOU? I'm worried about the DIRTY stuff too: especially since it seems to me it's getting more and more important to make one's I don't mean political I mean PHYSICAL stand clearly. You know? Reading Artaud again oh oh. I've been teaching, well I have nothing to teach on that surface it's all a farce, but otherwise, otherwise what a mine mind! Reading Artaud again with a precision because now everything, given the classroom and maybe this is all it's good for, everything immediately comes back at me-mirrors- is this what language is? The Art Institute gig (where I'm teaching) has been extended through the winter and I can see how via the students, I have NOTHING to do with any of the faculty or administration and God knows why they extended my gig, me the autistic catatonia of all ages, all porn, but they got equipment, so maybe I can hustle some pamphlets through, books! Will tell you more about this as progresses: have big underground plans. No more literature: just anything DISRUPTIVE. Always via words. Nice to know that Auster's not as uptight as I found him when I met him- but that was an uptight and quick situation, as I remember, as I remember. Oh dear, I want to write you so much, but I just wrote Glenda, and now I'm tired. Haven't done my own writing for the day, I'm grabbing time with this teaching, and I'm hot to trot so to speak, more and more I see: back to dream (there:narrative:here) here; the not separation but precision: how does causality work in a dream? The same way. So that space (which is beauty) we deal like Artaud with precise mental definitions occurs (meaning, is). Meanwhile, me, I make out in the front of a car with my boss while his kid sleeps in the back. Oh, Paul. Whoever gave each of us this kind of life? I don't understand anything thse days: this is my new mentality: and there are lots

One day Daphne arrived in town. It wasn't Daphne, but I'm going to call her that, because life is so confusing in any case. We made friends, she befriended me. She had friends, but I didn't get drawn into that circle, as it wasn't a circle any way. We started our own circle, or should I say course. The two of us, then some more. A new green field of language. It was a friendship that seemed natural. Straightaway we started writing to each other. Now I wonder if it was all a dream.

Last night I had a dream that confirmed it was all indeed a dream. I was wandering in a large building, going in and out of rooms where my students were talking. I knew it was a dream because they were discussing serious matters, not money and fashion.

I am looking at the Bellmer on the wall. I saw it move. Rose was staring at her belly, a ruptured wall, but she knew what she wanted beneath those layers. The green night was to be opened, no stone to be left unturned. To unbrick the prison of language that imposes on all our bodies. Caught between his act of drawing her and his act of making the engraving. The time of my birth. Even though the image was not borne into a public arena until 1966 when I too was borne into real life, the walls that had imprisoned me being dramatically ruptured. And then found by me a few years later as he lay dying, days from, in Paris.

Oblivion does not exist in the sense it is understood, I was told. Matter can no more perish than mind.

The walls opened onto a different perspective. I could see that I was standing there. All was me. The procession of people were all me. In various guises. There was no use in using a separating apparatus. The yolk and the whites were to remain as one.

Nothing. I can't find anything. Tirelessly I joint together the broken threads of a tapestry that at the same time unravels itself, so that the pattern can hardly be discerned.

Flaubert discovers both the terrifying freedom of the writer, the futility of claiming to express original ideas, finally the impossibility of writing which only comes from silence and which similarly moves towards its own particular silence.

of giggles. Will do rock song, my time has just been not, but Monday is last teaching day for a month, then to LA for four days, then find somewhere to live in this town because I desperately need a home, and all my books, to work, I'm still sleeping on a floor then then then poor head. Poor guug head. No no just dream. Am reading Nerval. Only when there is integrity, and, of course, you're right: the lust of politics, or else it's not that it's doesn't mrean anything but politics is what it is: disgusting. Only integrity. Am I being clear? Well, the porn feels good to me and as they don't say I try harder. Will be at above address for a while. And in Europe in May! Oh do write. HONEYMOON KILLERS is playing at nearby theatre!! I go again soon!!! I'm too tired for anymore of this and need to go back to Artaud but I love and think of you. K-

If I am alone I pretend to be two. As two I pretend to be three. After that it becomes too difficult, even with several windows, several mirrors and the whole panoply of language. With more than three it is best to pretend to be me alone.

Are these the rules from which we must proceed?

Do you remember *City Limits*? I have nothing to do with the future. Writing, along with living, is right now. Writing is the making of pleasure, as is living, as is death. They want me to take all the violence out of my writing. They want me to take all the sex out. They want me to take all meaning out. They want me to remove the language. And then they send in the anaesthetist to make a TV show on me. No wonder nobody ever kept a video of it.

Oh so pretty, pretty in pink.

Each of us must use writing to do exactly what we want.

Trying to pierce the darkness. Sometimes a moment from that night would light up for him, like a forgotten word spoken again. He felt as if it were a stone beneath which something terrible was buried. As if in a dream, he struggled agonizingly to roll the stone aside, but it was as if it were giving way in every direction and yet not moving.

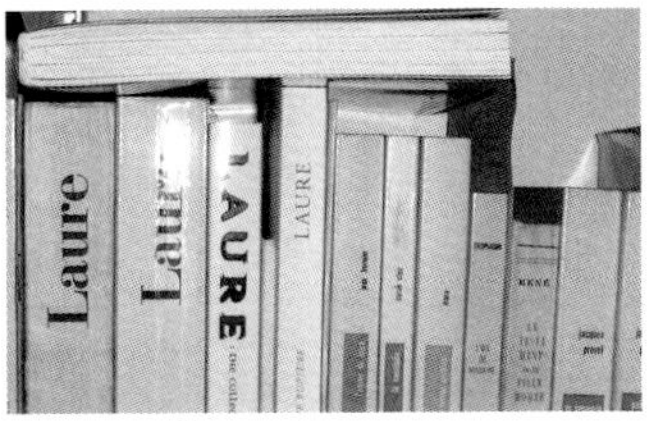

I don't want to dream anymore

There is a nervousness, an uncontrollable trembling, that is a hysteria, that thrusts itself at me, as I burst towards the one who explodes at me. And my mind does not shatter, does not liquidize. My mind is a stone, a stone wanting to be unturned. In a water that is borne of despair, cradled with despair

In this darkness I see the white, only the white, whiteness. In these screams I hear only silence, silence alone. Silence.

RESOURCES

Aurélia: Gérald de Nerval (trans Geoffrey Wagner)
Ghosts in the Mirror: Alain Robbe-Grillet (trans Jo Levy)
Topology of a Phantom City: Alain Robbe-Grillet (trans J.A.Underwood)
My Death, My Life by Pier Paolo Pasolini: Kathy Acker
The Maimed: Hermann Ungar (trans Mike Mitchell)
Interjections: Antonin Artaud
Lettres à Colette Thomas: Antonin Artaud
Le Testament de la Fille Morte: René (Colette Thomas)
Blows and Bombs: Stephen Barber

(CUNTS JUST WANT TO BE CUNTS)

Marc meets Carlo in the Psychic Brothel after the police interview: "I remember the whole thing differently now. It seemed a more expressive-cathartic thing than William Burroughs or Brion Gysin, almost like a despairing exercise in the futility of psychotherapy, experimental writing and the avant-garde to have any recuperative or transformative power. It was a writing of irrepressible powerlessness. All the S&M fantasy games suggested post-transgressive libidinal burn-out, you know, the failure of these creative-life modes to effectively counter the nullifying-robotizing power of *The Empire of the Senseless*. At about that time I dreamed I was cycling home through Hyde Park and I had a vision. It was 1994. The Spanner case was in full swing and the Ritual Satanic Abuse Panic was making prime time news. I saw plumes of smoke in the distance. As I got closer I could see that the city was in flames. Apocalyptic rioting had begun and the city was slowly being raised from the core outwards in a slow wave of total animal night violence. On the outer fringes, before me, a large group of leather clad S & M'rs were joined in a mass ritual. I asked them what they were doing. "We are preparing to channel the coming wave of human brutality - the dark night without hope – into a benign consensual form of sexual subordination and domination".

"I don't think that's going to work", I said, and cycled off into the city".

Being in prison is being a cunt. Having any sex in the world is having to have sex with capitalism. What can Janey and Genet do?

RED

Kathy is very ambivalent about S & M. She enjoys it a lot. She loves to parade her bruises to the middle class scum at the gym. But she also believes S & M is a product of American Capitalism. Descartes, she claims, ruined France. S & M is a product of the split between mind and body. Kathy is confused. She doesn't know how to be in love. She wants to take this S & M capitalist robot sickness to end of the night.

'Once upon a time there was a materialistic society one of the results of this materialism was a 'sexual revolution'. Since the materialistic society had succeeded in separating sex from every possible feeling, all you girls can now go spread your legs as much as you want ' cause it's sooo easy to fuck it's sooo easy to be a robot it's sooo easy not to feel. Sex in America is S & M. This is the glorification of S & M and slavery and prison' (KA)

K writes from a politics grounded in the sexualized and gendered body, from Artaud's b/w/o up-down, she seeks a writing-voice- (anti)-form that is pre-political/post-political/anti-oedipal as a challenge to the normative-sexual-political world of capitalist and patriarchal domination. But can there be such a thing as libidinal autonomy? How to outmanoeuvre the spectacular bio-social programming of the sexed body-subject.

By the time of BLOOD AND GUTS the literary text had come to be understood as an analogue of the social structure and the power relations that maintained it. To fuck up the conventional structure of the novel, to transgress writing conventions and to plunder, parody and abuse the cannon were acts of literary rebellion. Writing had to be HARD to read, but not necessarily hard to understand ("I never understood a word of Lacan" - K).

BLOOD AND GUTS is an exemplary case of post-structuralist literature. It is writing that knows about the interrelation of literary structure and social structure, of the relationship between elements in language and their relations in society. It knows that POWER and LANGUAGE are inextricably bound, and that this bind is a kind of WAR.

It is a SEX WAR.

'**Mr Fuckface:** You see, we own the language. Language must be used clearly and precisely to reveal our universe.

Mr. Blowjob: Those rebels are never clear What they say doesn't make sense.

Mr Fuckface: It even goes against all the religions to tamper with the sacred languages.

Mr Blowjob: Without language the only people the rebels can kill are themselves.'(KA)

K's confusion about S & M is mirrored in the conflict between a demand for precision in writing and the refusal of sense. K wants to state it is exactly as she can. There is no contradiction. One can be precisely contrary. The precision is in the language, in the statements, not in their logic or reason. Wresting language from its masters - Daly. Taking the language back. Stealing it and perverting it. Fucking it out of shape. But how do you fuck the master signifier out of shape? Desire is the complex plane of impulse and articulation upon which social and cultural systems are constructed, negotiated, fought.

Each of us must use writing to do exactly what we want
Every mirror is set against the edges of blades
We are sharpening the blades of defiant revolt

In 1981, I invited Kathy and Robert Duncan for lunch. They had not yet spent any time together, but Robert told Kathy that he had saved her Black Tarantula mailings because he knew they would be valuable. They set about charming each other: they talked about Charles Olson—important to both–Bataille, Hawthorne, and of course Robert was an old citizen of the magic universe Kathy would enter. When Robert left, Kathy swooned–He's wonderful–and advised me to have sex with him.

Robert Glück
April 2004

Dear Paul,

Just put my new typewriting ribbon in, after a month delay!, been writing by hand, and here it is! So boootiful.... I sqw HONEYMOON KILLERS again and was just shocked amazed how powerful...the blackest of the black... as it is... is this lousy Celine (I mean the letter?) my friend Bob Gluck who saw it with me, at he Roxie here in town midnight, we were both in shock couldn't talk afterwards: the movie makes/ shows language to be impossible...a day to recover... oooh I'm ocld , I'm back (I just put on a T-shirt, over that one huge man's man's huge blue shirt stood over heater in floor of hallway, pissed). Writin you is celebrating new typewriter ribbon. I've been writng by hand last few weeks, once stopped teaching went deeply as I haven't been (cause of teaching which makes me public, I think until I'm very strong that BEING PUBLIC means CONFORM, but I'm reading Nietzche right now, he IS the one who defines what's happening if anything we need to deal not with Marx' Freud's, all dead, but with how to move, post-Nietzche. ECCE HOMO makes me laugh.) So I stop teaching, (wherever my story was,) and zoomazoom the writng, all Propertius, scene bewteen Propertius and his girlfriend Cynthia who was, according to me like I'm some Latin authority hee hee, a whore, and they could only fuck when she was between tricks by diving into through windows deserted buildings that's what they do, of course my fav material (being) total schlock, oh I need some tea, the typewriter wire just came alive and scratched my leg...now the tea's brewing, and Propertius of course after the affair's all

Orange as Red

Kathy A, a young innocent seduced by Dickens, a writer who sought her out in connection with a headline-grabbing robbery she'd witnessed, is forced to leave home and seek work in the big city. Working in a sweatshop, she is befriended by Rosa L, a socialist determined to improve women's working conditions. Fired after a riot, she becomes a ticket-seller at a sleazy cinema. Unable to make ends meet, she turns to prostitution at a brothel run by Catherine Z, until it is closed after one of the girls is murdered by an up & coming politician posing as a collector for the Mob. Catherine opens a diner, where Kathy works as a waitress. There she meets X, who promises to make her a bigger star than Erica Jong, as Kathy lets it slip that she's really a writer and only working as a waitress to meet the right type of people. Catherine wants to be a star and go to Hollywood. Jealous, and working in league with Dickens, she shops X to the FBI, with the line that she recognizes him as the big shot gangster (his lookalike) plastered on the wanted posters all over town. X is gunned down, wiped out, in the glare of bright lights as he leaves a cinema set-up. Seeking revenge Kathy organises a bungled bank job, with a little help from some friends, escaping to New York and the big lights of publishing. Dickens, for his part, slips on a banana and crashes through a bookshop window.

Infernal

Rosa L learns from art dealer, J, that her apartment block was designed by Damien, a ominous myth-maker, for the three Queens: Flaubert, Proust and X. Rosa writes to her brother, Catullus, away in Rome, about her discovery. His girlfriend, O, seeks contacts who might shed some light, but is murdered sadistically before she can slip the bonds. Catullus returns to New York, only to find Rosa has been murdered by a mysterious group of downtown poets. No sooner does he find Rosa's friend, Lynne, than she is attacked by marauding artists and dies in a curtain call that becomes inflamed. Feeling quite fragmented, Catallus seeks J, the one who set these events rolling, who is then mysteriously killed after drowning some of his unwanted artists in the local sewers. Catallus stumbles on and falls into a maze of secret passageways in the block, all roads leading to Damien, who is

Kathy flew in from New York to have a dirty night with a cyberpunk writer at a motel in the Tenderloin. The next morning I met Kathy for coffee, and she said the people in the next room had complained about the dog. "The dog?" I asked, wonderingly? "That's weird Kathy, you don't have a dog...." Then it sank in that Kathy had been the dog. I said, "Oh no, Kathy, like Arf Arf?" And she replied, "No Bob, like Grrrrrrrrrr, Grrrrrrrrrr."

Robert Glück
April 2004

dissolve they always do, leads of course of course into Nietzche
because he too was up against the wall and if anyone's what do
I eamn? if anyone was ever up against the wall and whose work is
about (overcoming) that very thing it's Nietzche, and I need a
model RIGHT NOW! Which leads to the second story, and a apology,
but first the tea... one cup of apricot tea hot without milk,
because I'm on ampicillin again, the only ampiccillin junky in the wc
world, junk is supposed to start out being fun this is always
survival,: your (THE STORY) your friend Denis showed up N no
the day after Christmas' morning 8:00 when I was fucking
Howard. The circumstances here are Howard is my boss at the Art
Institute he is my only friend in this city I can really talk to
(I.E. talk art) I'm in love with him he has a girlfriend he likes me
I have to keep playing it cool not showing emotions etc. so he'll
keep seeing me (you get the power situation) this is the first night
I have him for the whole night (is sex owning?) we've been drinking a
all night are finally fucking I'm in my usual case of obsessive
nutty...: Denis rings the bell. I open door a Hindu cloth around
my tits nothing else. I'm obsessed with Howard. Denis looks at
me says your name. I didn't know I said "NOT now" "Come back at 11:0(
Denis wants to leave his bag. I think "Oh shit some guy probably
doesn't even know Paul and just heard my name, wants to crash, this
isn't even my place (I'm crasjhing, I finally have MY OWN PLACE
and can move in at end of January!!! will write address, first HOME
HOMEHOME in almost a year) Howard" I tske bag go back to middle of
fuck. Then Howard wants to go out at 10:00. I'll do anything Howard
says. I make him wait till 11:00,no Denis, we go out, Denis
shows up while we're gone and Denise says I'll be back, Denis

rigged to a support machine that keeps him painting. Catallus pulls the leads and finds himself confronted by Flaubert and Proust, in the guise of Rosa and O, breathing brimstone and venomous words that encase and cast them to hell, while Catallus escapes by the skin of his shiny-white teeth.

13 Moons is not a good year for it

Catallus has been to X for a sex change, reappearing as Kathy. Meanwhile, the object of her/his desire, Pierre, has disappeared to pastures new, leaving Kathy to be kicked around like a bitch by every man she encounters. Rescued by a hooker, Cynthia, she is encouraged to delve back into her childhood in the orphanage to help resolve her anxieties. Après a media exposé of her life story, Kathy seeks Pierre, who fails to recognize her, though he accompanies her to a flat where he falls immediately and helplessly in love with Cynthia. Distraught and with no one to turn to, Kathy commits suicide within reach of the lovers in their bed, a record jamming on the player.

Immortal

After a car crash, Cynthia suffers amnesia and recognises nobody. Taken back to a flat she shares with Desire she keeps silent on her loss while she seeks to rediscover her identity and her life. When a publisher contacts her and asks for more tapes, she discovers she was in the process of writing her autobiography. With the help of the tapes she unravels her convent background, and her chance meeting on an iron bridge with Desire, who introduced her to a world of high-class art prostitution. Her career as a call-girl is successful, until the day she meets Propertius, a classics art hero, in a hotel bar. Quitting her calling, in the name of love, or trying to anyhow, she is betrayed by Desire, who sets Propertius up as one of her clients. Despite her efforts, she is unable to escape the gallery system when the 'madam', called X, for convenience, lures Cynthia's teenage sister into the business. To save her sister's fall into degradation, she abandons Propertius. It was at that point, after an afternoon of taping her life story, that the car crash occurred. To provide a neat ending and bring the story in under 90 minutes, Cynthia does a deal not to finish the book in exchange for not writing about X, and for allowing both herself and her sister to escape from the clutches of

doesn't show up again. I'm really sorry. I would have been better later than 8:00 in the morning when I'm always dead plus Howard I was crazed, well the end of the story, besides my real apologies to you and Denis do write me or give note to person next time I felt and felt bad, is all my work I come homwe New Year's Day from Art Institute aparty stomed and drunk and I've been being good these days getting old mainly writing writing, of course through drugs more than usually insecure and wanting, call up Howard. Phine call doesn't give me what I want. I know I'm going to blow it. Go back to wiriting. This time there's boredom. I only feel boredom in times of want. I'm off-kilter. I call Howard again. I say I'm having trouble. He's sweet. He's ayutistic etc. paranoid names names ugh but never discusses anything but art as language for all else. No possiblity of emotional discussion. So I'm trespassing. I k ow I'm trespassing. I say I like you I don't know what to do with all my liking. He starts talking about me or girlfriend (immedia puts it in those roles) this sounds li ke soap opera. Your daily writer's writer's daily soap opera. He saw T.V. serial man leaves career girlfriend to go with woman who doesn't have career. I say "nonapplicable" but am very hurt cause implication is I can't be loved if I think. He says girlfriend is his grlfriend and he has room for only one. I say O.K. but am pissed so I hint girlfriend isn' maybe so faithful (he's worrying she'll find out he's been fucking me steady for month and a half). ((Matter of fact I know she's scewing some other guy a lot)) Well this is all soap opera and the wierdo it hurts. Of course I retreat from gossip and he's pissed and he'll not talk to me and there's goes ex more important firndship more important art-talk, just cause of lust mix-ups, and I hate myself OBSESSION OBSESSION OBSESSION I can't stop wanting to

prostitution and art commodities. Thus Cynthia slips back into the embrace of Propertius, etc etc

The Bogus Tower

Master criminal, Mr Plagiarism, recruits a gang expert in various forms of criminal irony. He holes up with them in his château outside Paris. His plot is to capture the Eiffel Tower, along with the visiting mother of the American President, Mrs Cripple, and hold them both to ransom for an inordinate amount of dollars. Unbeknown to Plagiarism, two of his gang, Jane Fonda and Anita Pallenberg, in the guise of Barbarella and Pseudo-Barbarella, are in the employ of D.I.S.N.E.Y. (Dicks in … you fill in the rest), a government agency that works against the government while all the time feeding the poor with one hand, starving them with the other, and using them for sex-slave trade as an afterthought. Having successfully effected his dastardly plan, Pseudo-Barbarella manages to escape with Mrs Cripple, even if slowed by her disability of running off at the mouth, and slobbering, as well as her inability to run fast. When Plagiarism sees his plans are going up in smoke, he primes the detonators on the Eiffel trifle and flees with half the money paid to date (a fucking large amount in anyone's book! This one included.) Cruising down the Seine, like a baddie out of a Bond movie, he is pursued in fact by a fake Bond actor (better known in his heyday as X), who reveals his hand, previously gloved, to show the scars made by his teeth after the excruciating pain he received a few years earlier when Plagiarism blew his wife and child sky-high in a bobby-trapped vehicle when he was working for the Counter-Espionage group called G.R.O.P.E. (which stands for nothing but groping… at plot). Meanwhile, Barbarella reveals her health-freak powers and flits around the icing on the cake to find the bomb and defuse it. Meanwhile, Plagiarism hasn't gone far. The escape helicopter that lifts him to safety is in fact infected by Arnold, head of D.I.S.N.E.Y., who charges him with everything going under the copyright laws. This is not a comedy by any means.

Thirsty Generations

From his office overlooking Berlin's city centre, Peter ABC, oversees his empire, unaware that Denise K, his secretary, is involved with a secret terrorist group, comprising her husband, Peter DEF, Arnold, a banker's wife,

deal with him: the crux of Western sexuality really is that Oedipal tie: what you most want is what you most can't have: THE HEAVY TRAINING. Artists are just clearer than most people. Oh Nietzche help me. What would sex really be like?

So here I am in this desert. Again I say I feel bad about Denis. You've got to write me, give a note, or call me the next time. My phone number if you don't have it is (415)285-4076. The new address (if everything works out in two days) will be: 70 Langton St., SF, Ca. 94103. But you can always keep sending letters here (I'm also using this as mailing address). For I'm often in the midst of some wierd obsession, and then to stop, because I do hear the sound of friendship, oh how does one deal with obsession, I need to see note. Etc.

I did send FLORIDA. Will send another xerox as soon as I get mt stuff (don't have copy here). That should be a few weeks. when I move into new place. Too bad you say late Russ Meyer. His early stuf: is MUCH BETTER. The epics. Much funnier. I feel knackered too. Up against myself these days. Talking to a friend yesterday, started talking about my work Nietzche, which I usually don't do I'm very private about what I really care about except to some few and then I say everything I guess that's why Howard hurts, I start talking about Nietzche, she says who, just the beginning ideas like no system etc., she says oh like Ursula LeGuinn in THE DISPOSSESSED (or something) an island that has political anarchy, I think what th fuck who needs someone to talk to , anm I an elitist? So I'm up against my own loneliness. The more together I get, the worse. The main is to be honest. Oh I hate this yucky so serious ugh I'm going to eat out at French restaurants. Give Glenda a big kiss.

Barbarella, a teacher (aka Bob), Clifford, a Virgin record store employee, Sarah, a junkie, and Flaubert, their recycled leader. Meanwhile, Peter DEF's father, Friedrich N, a high-ranking police officer, who is having an affair with his daughter-in-law, Denise K, (aka Kathy), is keeping the group under surveillance. Flaubert recruits a new member, Paul, an experienced terrorist, and moves him in with Barbarella (who could actually be Jane). They fuck like rabbits, but with the violence of human beings, preferring to visit underground S/M clubs when not reading Bataille, Guyotat or indeed Thomas Bernhard. All the members have extremely fractious family lives away from their terrorist cell life. Paul, out for a few shots of whiskey in a bar, is ambushed and shot on a tip off from Flaubert, jealous of his relationship with Jane, plus the fact that he, Flaubert, is in the pay of Peter ABC, if not his lover. Life starts to become complicated, and everyone takes on new identities that they constantly change, making it unreasonable to keep a track of anything. Terms like desire, timelessness, spread wide, romance, morality… come and go at will. Ideas come in one door and leave by another. Philosophy has its day. And at night 24-hour shops are visited to replenish their stores. They plot to kidnap Peter ABC, which triggers Flaubert to systematically expose each to Peter DEF. Sarah is one step ahead and overdoses. Others are killed going about their daily routines. Flaubert is defrocked, but nobody knows about it. Those left standing decide to make a film about their exploits, or at least script it for Hollywood blockbuster potential – they have an agent who is in touch with X – even if they have to rewrite it endlessly until it is drained of all life.

Don't Open the Attachment!

Disturbed photographer Denis… what the fuck is he doing there?! DELETE

Textaphobia

X, a writer with artistic ambitions, is obliged to work for Ecce Homo, a pornography publisher, in order to pay fashion bills. After toying with several random fantasies, including one in which a nun dominates and humiliates a pupil, X settles on a character named "Talk Art" modelled on a girl who undresses before the window in a neighbourhood apartment. The story is intended to be a sensitive soap opera of a convent-educated woman

This is turning out to be a ridiculously long letter. Read THE SHINING by Stephen King. It's shit and lots of fun. No wonder Burroughs loves it. Plans are: I'll be in Europe after May 6. Some possibility I'll have to be there before, I'll know in a few months. Am definitely teaching till April 1. Give Glenda big wet kiss. All my love, K-

P.S. Of course I forgot business. Will get tape to you of last chapter or something plus page for our TIGHT LEGS collab. (propertius material will be perfect) within wee.k. Oh this typing. It's late night. Just let me work a little on getting Propertius in shape, it's only first draft. I AM working HARD. Will senda al: SOON SOON

love

who becomes aware of her cunt in the course of her nightly excursions. Ecce Homo tells X to forget about 'art' and 'obsession', but also argues the importance of these elements to paranoia. As the story unfolds, it becomes the tale of a young filing clerk, a model employee by day but who solicits rough trade by night. On one nocturnal trip to a desert, Talk Art picks up a philosopher and fucks him in a toilet. At work the following day, she comes across two secretaries role-playing in the boardroom and is compelled to masturbate. That evening, Talk Art makes love with a woman whom she meets in a health food shop. Now only in need of an ending for the story, X becomes acquainted with the girl on whom Talk Art is modelled and they fuck. The next day, X realises the story must end with Talk Art being driven to the lower depths by her depraved sexual desire, imagining an encounter in which a policeman subjects her to brutal anal intercourse. The 'curse' is lifted and X 'allows' Talk Art to marry her boss SOON SOON, who has been conforming her throughout our story.

RESOURCES
Monthly Film Bulletin 1980

Dear Paul and Glenda,

Letter sna d the stuff for you Paul coming soon. I've I'm working on it and it's taking longer than I thought. Have been in the middle of moving, finally permanent place (ha ha) in two weeks I'm back on the road: thoughts yesterday while walking down night Mission bum srtreet only me and bums on huge deserted me in leather now top of hair bleached I'm going to be 34 most women my age babies and husband what happened to me here all alone I walk anywhere with the bums not a bum why do I feel at home here) so on the road, San Diego maybe NYC but I'm pissed at Diego who gave me a gig and is now cutting money in half) back here for these parentheses land anywhere 5 week teaching gig then to NYC May 6 gig then I'll be in Europe! A vacation? So here's new work, or new part of GREAT EXPECTATIONS, I can't keep work in mind anymore just what I'm on each section I'll figure it out or it'll all figure itself out sometime in the future I always rely on the future cause the present yuck usual run of disgusto affairs but less sex than usual I'm in gay town even going out with a girl tonight and everyone here coupled boredom actually more and more I just care about the writing and want people to TALK to KNOWLEDGE such an egotism-filled note I'm typing at a huge desk over which sun is pouring and I've been eating too much lately are people really breaking up ther there? oh everything's so hard why do anything and me back to Bronte James lovelovelove

New address; 70 Langton St., SF, Ca. 94103

I hate and love. It beats me why, but that's what I feel being done to me. I ache. I always ache.

So the story is still on to leave, to come across. For a vacation is a good excuse. I go everywhere for a vacation, even if it is a tour. Only by continual movement, perpetual movement, can I keep moving within. I want to settle down but I want to keep moving. So I will come to Europe.

Do I have any other stories to tell? I need to eat well, to have hearty meals. Size is everything. Size is not everything.

But I need to be pleasured well if I'm to pleasure well in return. And I am good at pleasuring. I need a sacrificial feast.

Tea. I live by tea. Coffee spreads darkness. How can one drink tea in another's home, let alone in a public place? Tea is a refined drink if it be savoured well. Though I can endure a tea that is not right, even if I don't like it. Coffee is just foul if it's not to one's personal taste. If all fails, try cocoa. Or a chunk of chocolate to melt in the mouth. Belgium chocolate, naturally. From there to Paris. Where culture breathes more than elsewhere. Ever the romantic.

When I'm on the street here, looking at the bums, I know I am one of them even if I do not want to live with them. I am confused. I want to be elsewhere, but where there is a here-ness in that elsewhere-ness. I want comfort. I want affection.

I am the vagrant come out of the extra-vagant.

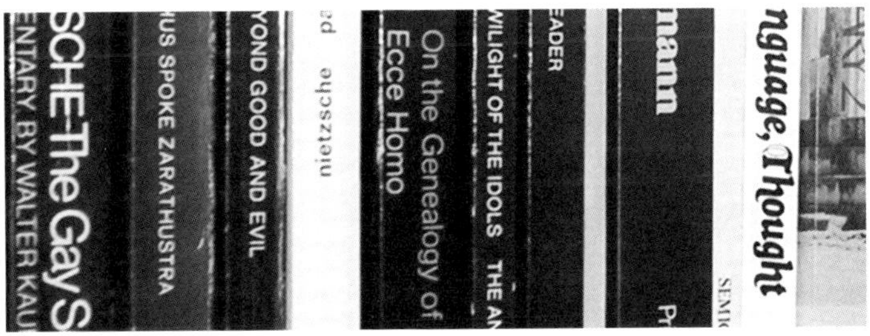

RESOURCES
Catullus (trans Ezra Pound)
Ecce Homo: Friedrich Nietzsche (trans Walter Kaufmann)

Cloned Pet to Fresh X

Marc goes to see Carlo. Carlo's mother answers the door. Once she was an actress, a famous one. But now she's a haggard lush. She shows Marc her photographs. But Marc isn't interested. "Where's Carlo? I need to see him". "I suspect he'll be with his 'friend' she says. "Sit down Relax a little and tell me what you've been doing". The mother strokes her hand across Marc's thigh. Marc shudders. "I hear you witnessed a murder. Is that true?".

"Yes. I mean no. I mean I can't remember exactly". "Tell me about it".

"Well, I was in this classroom, high up in a building which looked over the city. It was London but it was some future Blade Runner London, LA-style future-noir, at night. Here and there orange and blue flares were burning. The room was high-tech modern

with rows of tables around which a dozen or so students were sitting. I must have got myself roped into one of these museum-education programs.

I look out of the window...what am I talking about?...I can't remember. I must have begun to say something...I must have been talking about something.

I had a picture in my head...a big drawing-diagram thing, on paper. Something about machines, functionality

[EVERY POSITION OF DESIRE, NO MATTER HOW SMALL, IS CAPABLE OF PUTTING TO QUESTION THE ESTABLISHED ORDER OF A SOCIETY; NOT THAT DESIRE IS ASOCIAL; ON THE CONTRARY. BUT IT IS EXPLOSIVE; THERE IS NO DESIRING-MACHINE CAPABLE OF BEING ASSEMBLED WITHOUT DEMOLISHING ENTIRE SOCIAL SECTIONS']

I was going to say something about the depoliticization of structuralism in the Anglo-Saxon world in the 90's, how its techniques became 'methods for applauding the society and social values of American postindustrialilization'.

At one point I made a stupid mistake'. 'I' - the fucking lecturer - spoke of an important idea as if it was an obvious-trivial, throwaway thing. I denigrated the idea with the tone my voice. Did the very thing I'm claiming to criticize. The cheap and stupid trick of a prick.

But I can't even remember what the idea is. A boy with cropped-bleach blond hair responds as if to say..."well, if you don't think it's important why should we".

He looks like a younger version of the guy who gets his face pulped in *Fight Club*. I know his kind. I get angry...I'm spilling over...Can't remember what I said. I was angry. I wasn't thinking. Told him if he didn't want to be here then he should leave. He shrugged obstinately. Your problem mate. " Get out!" I tell him "NOW! I mean it. LEAVE! In fact ALL OF YOU. GET OUT! NOW!" By the time they're all filing through the door I'm screaming expletives. One of my 'colleagues' comes out of a room to the left.

To live by tea, three conditions are helpful: empathy, dexterity and experience.

You wrote to me about the difficulties of taking tea in another's home, let alone in a public place. Did I ever tell you about the time travelling in Japan when I came across a table set out under a tree, in front of a small wooden house? It was a tea-house, and as I knelt down at one end of the table the Tea Master told me the rules for taking tea there:

'Drink the entire portion of tea. It will not be large.' After I had been seated for a little while, talking with the other guests, the Master earnestly urged me to "Take some *more* tea." I didn't like to contradict him, but as I had been given none yet, I didn't see how I could take *more*. He replied that "it's very easy to take *more* than nothing," and so I helped myself.

'Be prompt in arriving,' he said. *'Eat everything served.'* This made me think of the teas at Manderley. Beneath the demure magnolias I was suddenly homesick for monstrous rhododendrons, slaughterous red, luscious and fantastic, rearing to the sky. I wanted to be elsewhere. I wished to be home, at four-thirty, punctual to the minute, where the door to the library would be flung open and the performance would begin: the laying of the tea, the silver tray, the kettle, the snowy cloth spread wide over the glistening wood.

Those dripping crumpets, I can taste them now. Tiny crisp wedges of toast, and

He seems understanding. They sometimes do. But I know I've blown my cover.
Couldn't cope anymore. Occupational hazard. I'll have to go. News of my 'crack up'
will soon get to the authorities. He shouldn't be allowed to teach here if
he's screaming and swearing at the students. If he can't cope he should do the sensible thing: cancel class, show them a movie, call in sick.
That's all I can remember. Now please, tell me where I can find Carlo".

"Yes of course, of course. But I have to ask why you're so interested in this murder business. You know the killer must be a maniac".

"Well if you must know I think I'm rather attracted to deviant pervert maniacs.
I can't help it. I have a morbid fascination for them. And if they're female, well, I go into rapture. You see I believe it is valid to consider women as possessing
a much greater capacity of experiencing their own bodies than men do. This means the existence,
in the female sex,
of a highly developed corporeal consciousness, with a greater and stronger
mind-body interaction. This fact is of great importance
for creative, artistic
and revolting practices because it predisposes women to an intense
projection of psychological conflicts on their sexual organs and correlated areas.
From the psycho-sexual point of view,
it also accounts for the very accentuated self-erotic
and narcissistic feature of female sexuality, resulting
on the fact that many women have, to a considerable extent, their own bodies as sexual objects for themselves.
This gives rise, in the female sex, to a kind of eroticism endowed
with a somewhat "centripetal" nature, of which women themselves are the "center."'

"Fascinating! I must say Marc, all this talk of maniacs and bloody murder has got me rather ... well... rather ...ready. Are YOU ready Marc? Are you ready to KNOW?"

She stares into his eyes and clutches his hands inside hers. Close up of her long black nails digging into his skin".

Marc shakes his hands free and jumps up. "Look, I really need to get going.
PLEASE! Now where is Carlo?"

"Of course, of course. I'll tell you. But I have just one last question. Why did YOU
become a pianist?"

Marc stares blankly out of the apartment window.

"My psychoanalyst says it was because subconsciously I was still in Westbourne Park, I hated my father, the art lad thing was getting big, floating over the canal. I'd been reading a lot of Burroughs, practicing meditation, various experimental writing techniques. Pressing the keys was like smashing my father's teeth in".

piping-hot, floury scones. Hard-boiled eggs. Cucumber and crab sandwiches, mysteriously flavoured and quite delectable, and that very special shortbread. Slabs of Belgian chocolate on a porcelain plate. Devil's Food Cake, that melted in the mouth, and his rather stodgier companion, bursting with peel and raisins. Peaches, fresh from the hot house. Vanilla pastilles. Jams. Preserves. Whipped cream.

Once, for a joke, Cora had herself served up on a vast silver dish – remember? – in a mass of meringue and rosettes and swathes of creams and sauces. Was it you or Paul who plucked the grape from her navel, and, with the utmost sang-froid, popped it in your mouth? There were always so few guests and enough food there to keep a starving family for a week, but I never knew what happened to it all afterwards: we ate little during those moments of bliss – mouthfuls.

'Each implement used in a tea gathering (including scroll, flowers, and food) has been thoughtfully selected by your host and has special meaning. They should be treated as objects of appreciation. Admire them and compliment your host with sincerity. You must be serious about it – not to be serious about meals is to be shallow. On an occasion of this kind it becomes more than a duty, it becomes a pleasure. This is the first responsibility of a guest – what the second responsibility is no one has yet discovered.'

Dear Paul and Glenda,

Sorry I haven't written back sooner I've been totally screaming at myself it's been if apologies are any good which they aren't and who gives a shit about guilt what was I saying? Now is no time not to write you cause I'm worried your last two letters: are you two O.K. I'm coming to Europe to see you. Even if I do have this new boy friend but he aint no boy friend cause he's got a girl friend in Japan who whom he's madly who gives a shit about grammar ?? in love with but nevertheless this NEW FRIEND hee hee treats me nicer at least for this week than the past three fuckers they all had girlfriends too what a town I'm going through the artists here so fast I'mll have to flee in two months or else back to some other pretense to hide the fact that celibacy is just another way of heartbreak. Is this called INSPIRATION. Fuck everything. So you two STAY TOGETHER well I don't know what the fuck I'm saying I mean I don't know what's going on I don't even know what's going on in front of me EVERYTHING's SO FUCKING HARD. WAR ON ALL FRONTS. But who makes decisions? Obsession. That's the only thing known. Person too. Known. Well I'm writing the two of you so I can write A REALL LONG LETTER and all it is so far is drivel. I'm worried about you two too. Sure everything shits. (I ain't feeling so bad today I got fucked well last night what a little obsession -relx from obsession will do.) And I'm having a good time cause I ripped off this paper (I sent you a copy) by sticking my own text over it and the paper-people being O.K. loved it so now there are some

I will come to visit. I will conjure wealth. Inspiration. Come to Europe. Give me enough of anything and I'll hang myself.

Jewels hang from my nipples. Or gilded breasts in Roman times, nipples gilded with gold leaf.

Art is making patterns for effect. We (The People Show) do that.

I love theatre.

Theatres of Rome were places for fucking, or fornication, beneath the fornices.

We (Laura and I) look to art for a meadow in which we can let our stronger passions turn around a little without our pants on. We like to see the fond grin fade off people's faces. We like to make our patterns with strong broad feelings. And we both think audiences can take it or leave it. We feel under no obligations to entertain although we feel considerable compulsion to forcibly animate people, by and large.

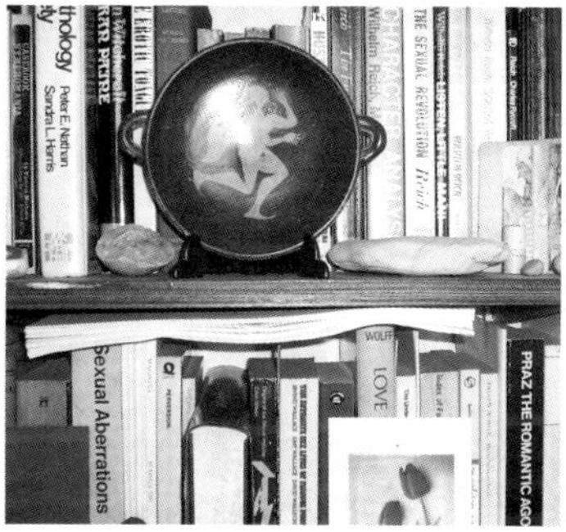

Now I am going to travel

Only the vulgar share a bedroom with their husbands.

Only the guilty share a bedroom with their husbands.

Only the desperate share a bedroom with their husbands.

Only the obsessed share a bedroom with their husbands.

Only the red share a bedroom with their husbands.

Only fish can share a bedroom with their husbands.

Only the me can share a bedroom with their husbands.

By and large, begin to begin

To face the mirror and innumerable pots of cosmetics. Athenian women used grease paint, antimony ore (mascara), red paint, white lead (as face powder), seaweed paint (possibly as an eye shadow), and beauty plasters (face packs). But in the rain, black rivulets flowed from their eyes,

people I can talk to here and not just old dead artists though I don't know if anyone reads too much but who wants everything (oh sex sex sex and time to work) but I only write Persian now I DON'T WANT TO WRITE ANYTHING ANYONE CAN UNDERSTAND catatonia hits. (I gotta see if my favorite soap opera's on)... here I am back again. Well, nothing is happening, don't know what this going away and coming back again is. Just like boyfriends. Am working on play for Richard Forman, from straight interview of Italian terrorist through Roman decadence to Persian no language. Came to me this morning. Very excited. Doing the Persian bit now. Should be ready by April, big performance with beats late April, in NYC in beginning May, then OFF. That's always the hope. I'm finally getting used to, escape except escape fantasies. Acceptance? Oh my god what a huge noise. I wonder if the building I'm sitting in just collapsed. Last week the winos set fire to it. And, not here, about three blocks away, a wino actually threw a bottle at me, not just a toss, a BAM, unuasual wino violence. Very crazy city this all extremes. Is hthat Buddhist? Does anyone care? I have tape for you cause I'm not a total lanme-brain just slow , I did this radio show for KPFA and it's good, but they're slow about making dub, they've SWORN in two days... And new book is out! is being shipped from NYC now! and then weill be shipped immediatement to you! and last night more people saying how wonderful HONEYMOON KILLERS is so I reply I KNOW GUY WHO WROTE IT I KNOW GUY WHO WROTE IT and I feel all wonderful and famous and for second not like total wierdo-schmuck (my usual). So lots of goodies to send to you soon and I love you I love you I love you Yes, you are right write about obsession. I learn. Eye? Oh this disintegrates into garbage? What should I read? Calder Puts out sweat from their cheek bore trickles of rouge down to their necks, while hair turned grey from the powder on their foreheads.

I have a trick of writing what I know of performers' secret problems into the script and constructing the show around them. In Nice Quiet Night *I did this for Laura and it worked to such a degree that Laura was crying for hours after each performance, but what a performance.*

Roman women treated their hair with lotions that made it shine like the midday sun, others dyed it reddish-yellow, considering natural colour ugly. Those satisfied with their black hair anointed it with perfumes from Arabia. Iron implements heated over a gentle flame crimped and twirled it into ringlets. Grey hair was plucked. Mesopotamians recommended as treatment for gray hair a mix of opium with a dash of the gall of a black ox, a scorpion, and a pig, all brewed with the head of a black raven and head of stork. Egyptians prefered a blend of laudanum, oil, cat's womb, and raven's egg. Once bald then to rub a salve made from fat of a lion, a hippopotamus, a crocodile, a cat, a serpent and an ibex.

Now I am going to travel.

It's a matter of cut and paste over society. That's the way to conduct oneself. But I'm getting fucking peeved at continually having to tamper with names, to stop from hurting people's feelings, after they done everything to hurt my feelings.

Cellotape. Remove. Or let fall off, over the years. Theory of art.

Write by thinking <u>against</u> the material. Since you don't want to <u>convince</u> self of your vision, etc. – but to let it be informed by the disintegrating now-moment.

Escape fantasies.

Inspiration.

Feel even more guilt.

RESOURCES

Sex in History: Reay Tannahill

Thoughts of chairmen me: Jeff Nuttall (1968)

Roman Day: Kathy Acker (another version of The End of Great Expectations, as cut and paste of a Research issue)

Ontological-Hysteric Manifesto 1: Richard Foreman

wonderful book from Russia called NOBODY. Wonderful. Get. I try to get Calder's translations of Russian and French...hard here. Desperate for new material. Now everything's catatonia Persian. Oh oooooooooooooooo

the me

"By using each other's texts,
we keep on living, imagining,
making, fucking, and we fight
this society of death,"

quoted Barbara Caspar,
across the lines from
Vienna, 2004

Cora is sitting at her dressing-table in a town house on the Rue de Chaillôt. Sometimes she nestles with a book on the window-seat, half-hidden by the laurel that stands in the garden. Its quivering leaves rustle like a silk dress. Some evenings Cora feels enticed to stand beneath it in her own satins, and the breeze whispers over them both. She imagines a woman insensible to love, a heart leaden to every pursuer, safely impervious, grounded; Cora wishes that she could stretch her arms and shoot forth branches. These are mutinous thoughts for a courtesan and so it is but rarely that she allows herself to stand in the garden.

From the windows of her bedroom Cora watches over Paris, and still feels a sense of surprise.

She was born plain Cynthia Ackroyd in Plymouth, was sent to school in France, and then returned to England where she lived as her grandmother's companion. Walking back from church one Sunday she was picked up by a man named Clive, who seduced her: she never went home.

When she was twenty-one, Clive took her on holiday to France. He had told her "I'm going to

Paris because in Paris no one speaks English. That's where I'll be able to make art." But Cynthia soon realised that she was far fonder of the city than the man, and jilted him. They rowed bitterly. "I am sorry if I hurt you," she said, as she left their hotel, "but I just don't see how I can become what the world calls a steady, prudent, virtuous woman. I'm afraid the time for that is long gone, even if I was ever made that way, and you of all people should know why. But the idea that somehow I like vice just makes me mad. I am not like the others. I want to be one of the vanguard people, and I'm going to distinguish myself by strict probity and love of truth."

Remembering his reply still sometimes causes her chest to constrict in the middle of the night – "You talk as if you had a heart. Women like you have no hearts! You don't have a heart in your body! You're hard – with your rouge and hundred-dollar-a-bottle polish who knows who you're preparing yourself for? You simulate beauty and you simulate love. You are bought and sold."

She didn't stay to hear more. She began haunting the bars, now calling herself Cora. Many prostitutes are foreigners, but she stood out even from the most exotic because of her short blonde hair. She looked like a pouty baby; it made her immediately popular. She was swiftly elevated from alley-treader to brothel girl, but never a concubine: only the vulgar share a bedroom. Once she had enough money saved, she found rooms of her own. She had a number of generous protectors, but no one special until Oscar, an artist.

Spread wide over Cora's dressing table are pots of cosmetics and brushes. Of course, all Paris has heard of her paintings, and flocks to witness her artistry at hiding nature, her skill at making patterns for effect. It is a performance. From the street below, the open curtains form a proscenium arch displaying Cora, seated in a kimono of embroidered red silk. Oscar stands at the back of the room, leaning against the door-frame, mostly silent. Cora believes he takes a professional delight in watching her.

CORA *(To the mirror. Putting on a hair-band)*

I brought to Paris the art of making up.

(She takes a bottle of foundation, pours a little on her fingers, and blends it into the skin of her face)

Some of the ladies of the theatre had the habit of retaining their stage make-up during the late evening, but with ludicrous results, for their faces appeared red or orange, unlike anything human.

(She applies concealer to shadows beneath her eyes)

(To herself, sotto voce)

Who was it called me *'une individualité à part, une spécimin d'un autre race, une phénomène bizarre et étonnant'*? ['Standing entirely alone, a foreigner or maybe an alien – a strange, astonishing phenomenon.']

(She takes up a box of pressed powder and a pad; carefully she pats it onto her face, contorting her features to reach every surface. Throwing back the shoulders of her gown, she dusts her collarbones and the top of her breasts)

(To the mirror again)

I had the idea that it should be possible to apply a lighter paint which would enhance the visage without making it ridiculous, and experimented at first alone, painting my face with tints of various colours, even including silver and pearl.

(With a selection of small brushes, she covers her cheeks, then her eye-sockets and brows, with brightly-coloured shadows)

I also used a dye from London to turn my red hair yellow. Soon I had requests from other ladies to show them the art, which I am pleased to do, and now I throw open my rooms for ladies and gentlemen to come and see me. I am at the height of my beauty, and it is only fair to admit that I look upon these occasions as times of advertisement.

(She applies two coats of mascara)

If coins are made to roll, and diamonds to glitter, I cannot be reproached with having perverted from their normal uses these noble things.

(A twinkle in her eye)

With the latter how I glitter, when the former roll my way!

OSCAR (Aloud - to Cora's eyes, which meet his in the looking-glass)

Mirror, my enemy, in which you are allowed

to see your eyes that Love and Heaven honour,

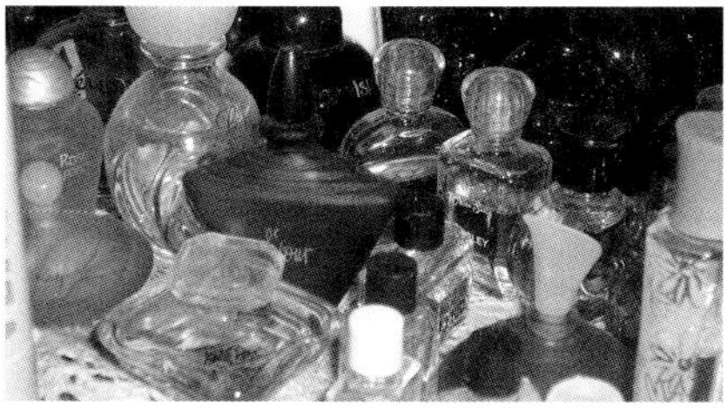

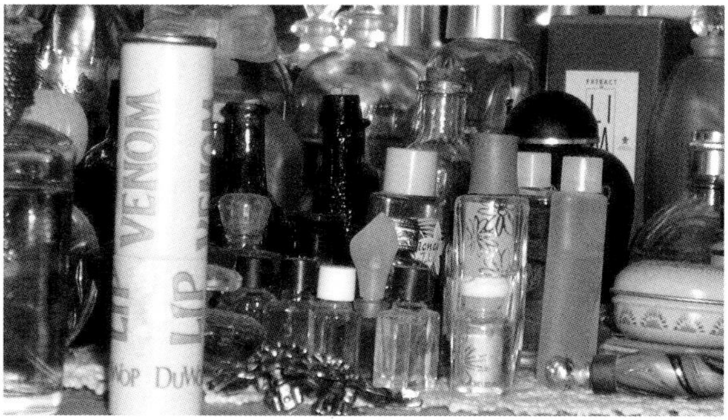
LIP VENOM

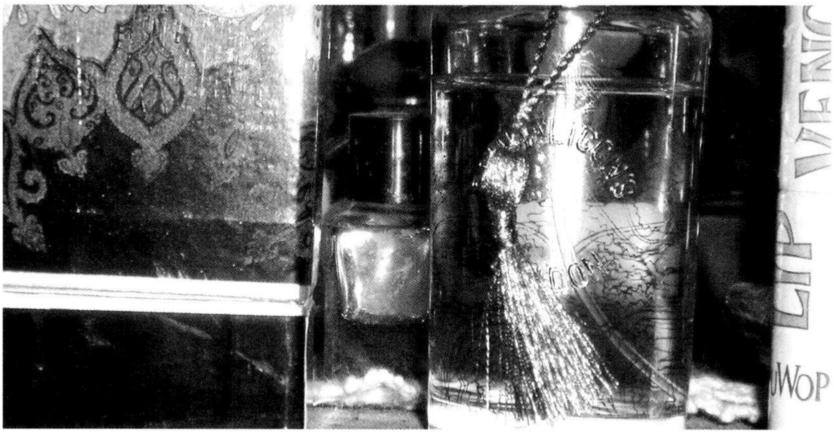
LIP

enamours you of beauties not your own.

(In his thoughts)

Play-acting again! Outlandish blue shadow around your eyes, like a woad-stained Briton or glittery disco queen! Is there no dressing-up-box you won't raid? And that fake tan - it's as artificial to the eye as its name to the ear! And as for your bleach bottle, you stupid girl - you might be blonde to the world, but one tug at your dressing-gown cord and I can reveal the truth!

Go back to your roots. I'd certainly not look at anyone else if only you'd let me see you more often. You look best in the mornings - no make-up and fresh from sleep. Stay like that in bed with me, and don't sit waiting for business any more, with that shop-front face on.

(Cora's eyes have not left Oscar's. Holding his gaze still she takes up a dark red lipstick but, instead of applying it to her mouth, she writes on the surface of the mirror:)

JE SUIS MAÎTRESSE DE MOI

(She smiles.)

Dear Paul and Glenda,

No, I'm not crazy (I don't think) actually I have no idea, I'm just overworked beyond and I don't know what beyond, and as a consequence very frazzled. I'm tending to overwork, especially with the teaching -the play for Forman, finishing up the last 'free' section of BLOOD AND no, I mean GREAT EXPECTATIONS, I AM going too fast and no cocke, coke I mean, cock by the way has been O.K. meaning I get it boy do I sound pig macho but it's the usual rotty boyfriend shit, actually I think I'm just into my own writing not writing so much as finding out too much these days to pay attention, which at least is also pay attention to the usually boring nagging pain, and I am getting middle-aged I'm going to be 34!, I thought 33 and then Peter (xzee ex-husband who by the way is doing the music for the Forman play) came in town, and said NO, HONEY, 34, not 33" so I'm going WOOWOO meanwhile I'm working (also) on this great magazine called RESEARCH (the old SEARCH AND DESTROY), and getting my class to do their own mag, cause they waon't learn anything and I don't know I ain't gonna be Miss Powermonger, they call STUCK, mee I'm stuck with too much work and gettting nervy and yelling crabbing at the brats they REALLY are bratty especially the guys I told them all they should take over the school and the women should take over from the males (no one liked that one- so much for my militant crabbiness: that's what I am a MILITANT CRAB) and three performances: one here and two in NYC one in NYC being : (hee hee hee) I'm supposed to deliver a paper at the, get this one, FIFTH INTERNATIONAL PSYCHOWOOWOO ANALYTTIC CONFERENCE, so I sent them thisripodff of THE STORY OF O though I LOVE Batalille, and they didn't crab at that one, so now that they've translated it into however

Production note: use of crab technique, sidewards.

A phosphorescent crab is seen crossing the stage. The map isn't resolved. Open closed.

I'm screaming...

How long did that silent play between him and the bust last? Had he really lived that scene?

You're a crab so you can tell me.

He was the one who ordered his own punishment, who suffered in silence and lovingly kissed the arse that oppressed him.

Awoke in a cold sweat to discover I am not I and I am no other than I.

What brought you to my bed? The dawn that was red.

Is my life being lost in laughter?

I need to descend further if I'm to discover what loving is, if I'm to discover the dangling thread that makes love possible. I descend. I awake in cold sweat. A state of unknowingness. Can I live in a mistake? Am I the consequence of a mistake? I need another sip of water. I drown in a sip of water. Obviousness is difficult to put up with. I am the world and its confusion. I desire pleasure as a meaning of life. As a method to attain life. I think this kind of confusion is inevitable. There is no beginning or an ending.

It shifts as you seek it, as you think you reach it.

When the impossible is stretched before me, and is still infinite, offering no means to attain an end, even though I know it will end, probably as soon as I've worked through the final letter, there is no certainty that that will happen, that something will not keep it going, even though a time limit is applied. But time can become a timelessness. And so the excuses for continuation are faced though not faced up to.

And as the story ends, or shifts and seeks an end, so the start. How much blood was spilt, blood dropping to earth, being absorbed? How much sleep was passed, when words and thoughts came and went, disappearing before apparent abruptness, that apparent desire to begin? In the beginning.

many kinds of babel, I intend (instead) to read only Persian again, I'm writ: writing ponly Persian these days except to loves like you cause I REFUSE TO NOT BE CATATONIC. How's that for politics. I just had this incredible dream- the second main dream of my life. Now I have to write it in Persian. So the first story, not the dream, which'll also be the end of the Forman play, is called ALI GOES TO A MOSQUE. But I've had to learn Persian to do it, so every sentence is a labor, forget love, I'm working too hard to be my usual desperate emotional turmoil, but here, (like Arabia? who the hell knows?) is a desert, one reason I'm working so hard is I know the second I get out of here and back to civilization I'm gonna gigggle for hours so I want to get everything done. Maybe outside-NYC (or whatever that is for you) is our modern art-Bedouin or Bedu society. Me-no society.

Don't know when I'll be in Europe. Was planning to come in a few eeks cause thought BLOOD AND GUTS would be out in France, but can't get definitive statement from Lemaire and Diego says I'll be in Milan in fall for his festival (if that doesn't fall through, he swears it won't) so everything's still up in the air. Plans as of now are: go to NYC may 1, app. see what happens. Will keep you informed. Tape has been done for weeks but this fucker from a radio station is delaying, four weeks now, getting it to me after I did radio show for him for free so as soon as he stops being a zombie... Speaking of which, I'm getting my Haiti woowoos again... Just want to get out of here! Sun!!!!!! What do I read? Couldn't get to sleep so giggled over Iris Murdoch about four last morning. Anything Persian. Huge sands dunes cascading over my head. Borges leads to dreams. Who cares about craziness? Wonderful new writer named Kis. Ukranian? That's all for now loves. Soon you soon see see oh, I hope! (even if I can't talk straight) love KKKKK (it's my birthday soon!!)

Scene: A train of thought.

Timelessness: Lost again.

Belonging: (*lifting the flesh*) Never.

The colours: Thoughts go back to that time so no idea why I use the word illicit. I was still positive.

Style: This idea makes me shed tears. Did it mean timelessness for the past?

(The real world rings.)

Darkness: I see her in the flesh of lightning, a flash in which she seems to rise up, as if through coincidence.

Wasted: Everything I have ever done in my life that you see is close to death, is close at hand, somewhere near this hour.

Darkness: I only replied in disjointed phrases. Green shutters feasting on vines. Belief that tears at events linked.

(*Exits.)*

A storm: I thought I saw a black sun in an empty chair struggling with the dangers of invisibility.

(Laughter. Incomparable.)

Ruins: One night I dined in a café off the Boulevard St. Germain. I was carved with fantastic patience. I do not understand myself. *(Understanding herself, pretending to.)*

Two perceptions: *(crazily, dressed in red, bust size 34)* During the night my delirium grew worse as I loved and trembled at the thought that defined itself.

Lips: *(parting)* At about eight twenty I was placed in a bath to shimmer and gratefully slid down the arm that I had exposed. Do you?

Larger then smaller: This thought reassured me, but did not free me from the fingering that was made more plausible by my obsessions.

The scene repeated: The universe from within.

Understand: *(firmly)* Over my bed I've hung my emotive clothes, only pale flowers now, and faded foliage, an existence perhaps that I was persuaded to accept.

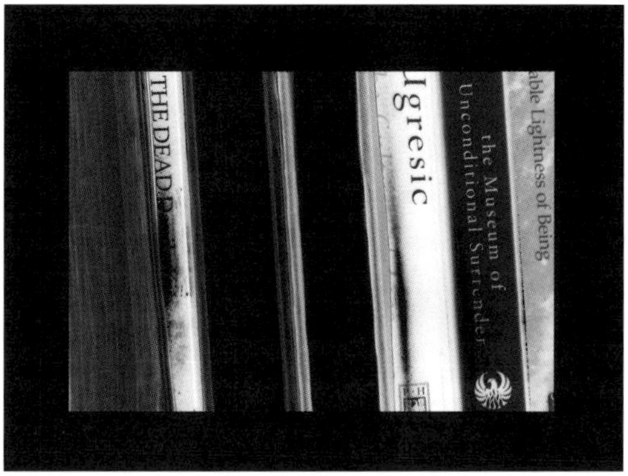
THE DEAD
the Museum of
Unconditional Surrender
Lightness of Being

(K, dressed in redder red, enters, with another text.)

Thoughts: And as the line of the shadow creeps behind desire we climb a recaptured sentiment without wishing to penetrate her cunt. *(K goes into the next line and closes the door.)*

Night: *(grasping an ankle)* A silver noun shines in the sand and even though there is meaning there they expect anger and scars.

Beam of light: That night my dreams were of dreams that took me to Paris. They seemed real and described fast circles.

Understand: *(sighing)* And where do you suppose you are now?

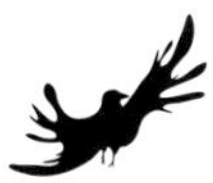

RESOURCES

Birth of a Poet: Kathy Acker

The Poems of Propertius (trans A.E.Watts)

The Book of Sand: Jorge Luis Borges (trans Andrew Hurley)

The Mirror of the Unknown: Danilo Kis (trans Michael Henry Heim)

Aurélia: Gérard de Nerval (or at least a dream of it) (trans Geoffrey Wagner)

I wake, my skin damp.

I dreamed of a white figure,
kneeling at water's edge,
curtained by hair.
Mesmerised by reflections.
A crack of twigs, a sudden
movement

● and dimples in the surface,
six feet out.

The shore empty now apart from a
man, who stands mouth open
still hidden behind a tree.

"She's gone, ain't she?" he says,
"She won't come back no more?"

I woke, with a feeling of falling.

When the angels fell,
some fell on the land,
some in the water. Those
on land became fairies,
those on the
water, sprites.

*I conceal my infinite self at the
bottom of the sea in the grotto
where the sirens swim, fatal to rash
visitors.Only you, and the loathsome
monsters seething in those black
abysses, do not fear me.*

Come with me to the ocean,
immense blue bruise slapped on
the body of earth.

Together we can descend further, as far as crabs and lobsters. They know the secrets of the deep. Let us linger together on the sands, that desert stretching beneath the waves. Even lovers drown, if wakened by human voices, but the siren-song will stop your ears.

We will swim in the sea of delight. Immersed and submerged in joy we shall feel no joy, for we will be joy itself. Join me in the abyss, profound, bottomless. Let's plumb the depths stretching before us. They are so nearly infinite. But which is deeper – the depth of the ocean or the depths of the human heart? Which is the more impenetrable?

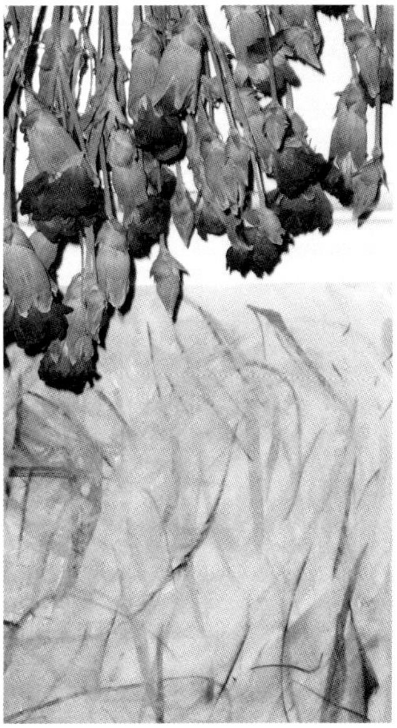

"This book is the most completely unified work of art you have yet produced. One that by its formal concentration and its unified shape at every depth of reading fulfills the sort of demands that Sterne or Canetti makes of the novelist."

Quote from Alain Robbe-Grillet for Great Expectations, adapted for use on jacket of 1982 first edition

70 Langton St.
SF, CA 94103

Dear Glenda and Paul,

Now I was going to write (type) Glenda and George. Why is that? With memories of Gilbert and George in mind? Living in dreams... No wierd life cause no way of telling. Today, yes back in SF, too much work had to finish up: crazy two weeks in NYC: all I had fled from, and I did flee, stupid Italian conference (on sex and language whatever those things are) where the Italians now (having the money, money is always the colonizer, no racism here) are now colonizing us, and I'm asked to 'give a paper' (why?) but at this 'conference' (everything should be in quotes) it's obvious I'm the token 'punk', no one speaks to me, except to give me instructions in French (who do they think I am?), so I say "I'll speak on the writings of J. Lacan" (cause I find Lacan absolutely unreadable) and proceed to lecture them in Persian, what do they think? and someone says, "This is M. Robbe-Grillet" so I say "Oh Oh I love your books" and he says "I do not speak English". Back in my hotel room, they give me a hotel room for this conference, they are paying $75 a day for this Holiday Inn style only worse mauseleum, and I think my mother half a block away from here herself alone in a hotel room suicided so I go crazy- that's the worse, then the next day, a benefit for Semiotexte where while I'm on the stage, reading Persian cause I'm catatonic some guy I think (if I'm getting the story right)

Unjust desperation, a story of parts. And parks. And puking

Back in the desert I get to reflect. There were so many women their limbs disappeared in the shadows.

I need to flee. To Algeria. But that only brings back memories, money pouring from them.

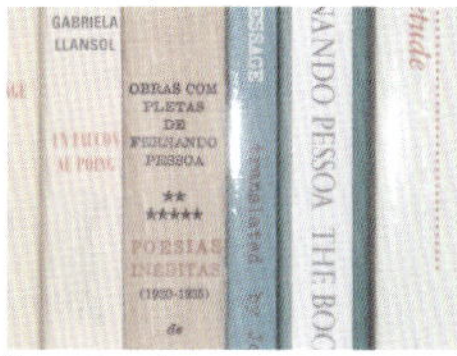

So we leave for Lisbon. Cos there is peace. Walking down Rua Augusta, ankles aching, having tripped over the cobbled back streets when Pessoa's men have stumbled their lives, victims of cirrhosis of the liver, alive no longer.

Her shoulders were bare when I walked in the room. She had intended pulling her blouse tight. Instead she rested her mind and let it slip. About to collapse in exasperation, for she had endured a terrible few days, excessive work, which was pleasure, but work nonetheless. She now perceived the degrees of heat the flat had generated. It was humid, no windows open, sun beating down on the Baixa, little breeze today to cool between her legs. She spread her thighs. Ran her hand the length of the right. The two rings inserted in her clitoris itched. She extended her hand, brought it back, couldn't reach the cream. She rubbed at the irritant, unable to move any further. A dress, she would wear a dress today. Time she went out. Time she had her body welded to another, to the male of her fantasies. Fuck fantasies. Reality. He is wearing a rough pair of trousers, as if made of hessian. Her skin was too delicate for that abrassiveness. She went with him. Only the word FUCK and the word CUNT was needed. Though she did say I hope your cock is going to fill me, thrill me, please my very being. But he didn't understand that torrent of words. There was little room for understanding on that front. She could feel his hands carressing her buttocks. He was the only man for her right now. There was no other. Nor did he look at any of the other women as they slipped off the main street and headed for his place. For a moment she thought they were headed for a group of men loitering in a doorway. She was being set up for a gangbang, or for them to be witnesses to the drama. These houses were so small, who could tell. She halted, he didn't. Or he did. There was a pronounced pause, before he said NO

cause he wants to make it in the NYC art world tries to piss in a bottle and can't and everyone thinks its part of my act. Later the same evening the last 'act' eats live mice and rats. The next night Sylvere asks me what I think of all this, I say "Puke. This experience with Italian conference etc. makes me realize the only viable thing/act is art. People were doing anything to try to get any media attention. Nothing shocks. Just desperation." He says "But Kathy, you have to play with the media to survive. Why do you always see content? You're a moralist." I reply, "No. I just want the freedom to do what I have to. The media, your set-up, doesn't allow this." So Semiotexte Inc. has gone to the pigs. And at the same conference my friend Kathy Bigelow who did the Polysexuality issue of SEMIOTEXTE sleeps with Bernard-Henri Levy. Then tons of friends, business, no sleep, another performance, all that goes on in NYC now is desperation or back to art: really good art. We're in life again! Th n I return here, tired, this desert!, say Oh Oh if I don't finish GREAT EXPECTATIONS now I'll never finish it, and while I'm doing that Peter calls and says Foreman's raising money on the play and needs it, so I say I'm about to collapse so I might as well finish everything before I collapse, so after 20 hours a day non-stop one very tired ex-writer who has no other life left and really can't gossip about anything cause there's nothing to gossip about no evil sexism no hurt feelings not even champagne has finished one novel GREAT EXPECTATIONS and one play, and one two-year portion of a wierd life. This one involved running away. What will happen next? My room's all tidy, so to speak, I loved the Ulli piece you sent me. Makes me giggle. All that jab language.

Call me 288.5454 K

VIOLENCE. I started falling into his arms. I don't sell anything. I sell all. This was such a luxurious room, she couldn't believe it was Lisbon. When had she learnt of the death of Daphne? It wasn't that long ago. Several days. She flattened herself against the wall and let his hands take their course. There was the noise of excitement in his breathing. When he found the two rings, he wheezed. A sharp hiss. Barely a greeting. He pinched them with his fingers. Pulled.

She had been pulled again.

Language chooses you. I am passionately devoted to life and sacrifice it only to literature. Literature, not literary circles, unless there are men to fuck there. I adore the multiracial babel of languages, a bastard culture made by the victims of those we have screwed. The walls of the buildings are covered with graffiti in Arabic that the Parisians do not understand but that I decipher with genuine delight.

With a piece of white string no doubt in a cross but the only part of the string that is visible goes round the book lengthwise the other if it exists goes round the side of the book is spread wide like open legs very precise in form pointing obliquely downwards at this precise spot in the marble of the shade and its glass spine the heavy red binding the big embossed letters covered with the same red velvety material and then the text with its three drawers.

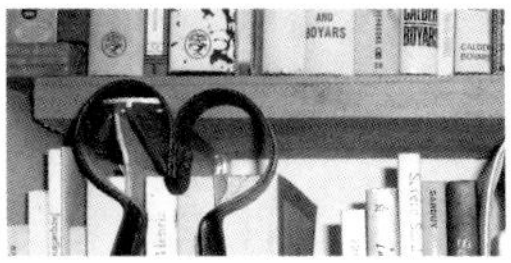

I said thank you to Monsieur Robbe-Grillet for the quote, though I fear he didn't understand my Arabic. But I knew that when I got to Paris I would find a future ally in Juan.

The book, like the space in which its daily bustlings back and forth are described, is vast and rich in possibilities; ramifications, intersections, connecting points, one-way journeys, roundabout itineraries, parabolas, half circles, ellipses, dead ends. To examine the mapping of the book is to yield to memory, to escape, to delirium; to accept utopia, fiction, fable: to visit the monuments, the abominations, the horrors of the text, one's own monuments, abominations, and horrors, without ever having to rise from the sofa.

The drama is a mirror stage. Or nor, the mirror stage is a drama. I can get that fare. The anticipation of the complete book. Or drama. Like two

3.

Stonehill still says they're doing BLOOD AND GUTS and the new novel will come out through City Lights distribution (my own money backing, what the hell, I need something new out NOW, my books are doing selling better than ever and they're so old I think they're dead) and I won some prize and who gives a shit no Babeth's not involved in RESEARCH I send you new copy and new book. Are sentences reasonable? M. Lacan? Mr. Logie is a pig: he's the guy who locked me up in Seattle. He's not exactly a pig, he's extremely schizo, totally wonderful and totally violent. I hope to avoid him. Will try to get free xerox of GREAT EXPECTATIONS and send to you. All these xeroxes and mailings are running crazy so I'm gonna try to get some stuff free somehow. Lost money on the NYC gigs in spite of having three, what the fuck, I worry and really every day I wake up there's food I'm alive shit what do people do when they don't write? What do they think? Do they think? I want a vacation!!! says this little pinky. Sun. Shall we go to the beach? How are you two? What goes on? It's been a long time since we've seen each other.... Will write again soon with more definite plans. Love love K--

sisters who knock up against each other bang.

{Forced perspectives
{Intentionality is all

ÉDITIONS DU SEUIL
27, RUE JACOB, 75261 PARIS CEDEX 06, TÉL. 329.12.15

SS/IW

Paris, le 26 janvier 1983

Monsieur Paul BUCK
4 Bower Street
Maidstone
KENT ME16 8SD

Cher Monsieur,

Portugal doesn't offer many resources these days for the hasty visitor eager to bring back slides with at least a touch of red.

Hasta pronto

Severo

Severo Sarduy

S. A. Cap. 6.250.200 F - Télex 600.605 - C.C.P. Paris 3.042.04 - R.C. Paris 542.057.724 B - SIRET 542.057.724.00016 - Adr. Tél. Ediseuil
20.012-6-81

{See below

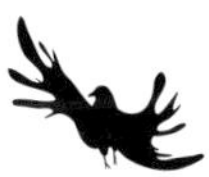

RESOURCES

Great Expectations: Kathy Acker
The House of Assignation: Alain Robbe-Grillet (trans A.M.Sheridan Smith)
Space in Motion: Juan Goytisolo (trans Helen Lane)
In the Labyrinth: Alain Robbe-Grillet (trans Christine Brooke-Rose)
Landscapes After The Battle: Juan Goytisolo (trans Helen Lane)

I found an old postcard from you. It just said: *'There's an old story, Daphne, a love song, really, that goes round in my head when you stand at the foot of the sycamore or under white laurels.'* You never told me which.

But whose song do you hear beneath the apple tree?

As an apple-tree among the trees of the wood, so is my beloved. Under its shadow I delighted to sit, and its fruit was sweet to my taste.

"Do I really seem to you worth the price?" Freia asks, apple blossom in her hair, offering eternal youth.

Give me life, rather, and death. Let his left hand be under my head, and his right hand embrace me.

My beloved spoke, and said unto me: *'Rise up, my love, my fair one, and come away. For, lo, the winter is past, the rain is over and gone. The moon putteth forth her silver apples, and the sun's golden fruit give forth their fragrance. Arise, my love, my fair one, and come away.'*

And then, the real Rebecca took shape and form before me and stepped from her shadow world

—like a living figure from a picture frame.

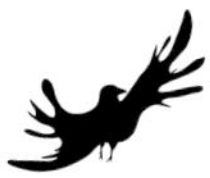

RESOURCES

Great Expectations – Kathy Acker
'Surrealism towards Comfort' – Fabienne Audéoud
Poems – Matsuo Basho
'Sunflower' – William Blake
Jane Eyre – Charlotte Bronte
Wuthering Heights – Emily Bronte
Lust/lust to write/to write out of lust – Paul Buck
Alice in Wonderland and *Alice Through the Looking-Glass* – Lewis Carroll
Songs of Maldoror – Isidore Ducass
The Hollow Men and *Whispers of Immortality* – T.S. Eliot
History of Sexuality – Michel Foucault
Crow – Ted Hughes
Rebecca – Daphne du Maurier
Poems – Gérard de Nerval
Metamorphoses – Ovid
Memoirs – Cora Pearl
Sonnets – Petrarch
Elegies – Propertius
Tea Poems – Sen Rikyu
Letters – Marquis de Sade
The Tempest – William Shakespeare
The Song of Songs – Solomon
Collected Works – Oscar Wilde
Memoirs – Harriette Wilson
Decrees of the Venetian Senate (1543)

Dear Paul- Isn't this card great? (Picked it up at a
gay S&M shop.) Lazy days here- work & not much else
per usual. Sorry I didn't write back sooner- had a
performance that took up my energy- now almost
everything tied up: Foreman has the play & loves it
(though he's not yet able to raise money on it), the
new novel's finished, performances basically over
(2 small ones in the next 2 months, but I can
weasel out of those), just waiting around for the new
novel to come out & then when I have ~~not~~ some-
thing new (I'm not a total failure, etc.) will be able
to get out. All new affairs over too, but what's new
about that? Getting older is wierd: realization
that life is maybe something to rejoice getting
away from, no root here, no home or person no
more to run to. More & more a traveller. Wish the
new book was out- will be about 2 more months-
so I could split- have had it with SF (now that
I'm getting on all these art committees- what a bad
joke.)
Is this letter too personal? Haven't written you for
SO LONG, for which I apologize- you know I'm
flaky- but I AM loyal- are you O.K.? I think
being a novelist in this falling-apart & dan-
gerously rapidly growing fascist world is nothing
short of insane. But I guess living is pretty in-
sane unless you make up lots of lies which is
what most people do. It really is getting strange
in this country: everyone wanting something
(again!) called NORMALCY & looking desperately for
it. Lot of reactionism (direct translation of
reactionism is fear). Am dying to get out of here.
But not unhappy: reading Beckett, he's so funny!,
working on new novel (already) a total non-
understandable cut-up of an Ambler novel- so
who gives a shit about the world. This spring
(over)

Let's put this under the general heading of: Lies or fiction? Or:

Framed in Guilt

It was fun to move to London in 1967, at least in spirit, if not in fact, as the blurb states. You see intentionality is all, as I keep saying, as David laid it on the line for me.

Farewell to Passion

I'm waiting for it. I'm waiting. I've forgotten. I'm forgotten.

My Flesh is Sweet

Good art…can't convince of anything because its method is to interfere with (undercut) itself. The task is to be with—equally—the impulse AND what interferes with, undercuts, stretches, tumbles, dishevels, scatters… the impulse.

Home is the Sailor

I've always wanted my art to be about *whatever it was that gave me the energy to make it.*

Strange Witness

To write before writing. To make the writing the preparation for writing.

The Big Kiss-Off

To escape through writing, or reading, or reading writing, writing reading, or writing writing reading, beginning again and again is a joyful thing even when it's a joyful thing to amble through the troves of train fiction, or to find something in those narratives. Paul's preference is to look beyond those Fifties pulpsters like Thompson and Goodis, to find a keenness in Day Keene, Harry Whittington, Gil Brewer, Bart Spicer, Vin Packer (OH VIN PACKER, OVERLOOKED OVERLOOKED)… and others. A preference to find a way into the criminal mind, not the detective mind, not the pursuit of resolution and incarceration. To disperse the clues, dissolution and disappearance.

Joy House

It's about the tapestry (many threads from many sources) weaving itself and reweaving itself. Each moment… a unit of joy coming into itself.

ran into whoops can't write here – P. Orage Genesis · what a sweetheart

bye-bye love

Kathy's "Birth of the Poet", directed by me at the Next Wave festival at the Brooklyn Academy of Music. The biggest scandal of the decade. Four nights in a row, all through the performance, the audience of 800 screaming back at the stage in response to the "obscenities" of Kathy's text set amidst what was an "opera house" sized performance. People not only walking out in droves, but throwing things (mostly their rolled up programs) onto the stage. And I remember on the first night – in the middle of the show, a white faced Kathy running up the center isle to where I was standing at the back of the audience – "Richard – my God, they hate me!" She exclaimed. "Why do they hate me?" I had no immediate answer. It was a great scandal – and finally, a great play also.

Richard Foreman remembering in April 2004 those days of the performance in December 1985

Things bleed in unexpected ways into other things. The theme is the "sequence of things", the theme is 'everything that wants to be written'—and how everything is secretly present in everything else.

Notorious

Understand—it ALWAYS makes sense. Sense can't *be avoided. If it first seems to be non-sense, wait: roots will reveal themselves.*

The Dangling Carrot

Did I tell you about J.P.? How did we meet? It was something to do with The Honeymoon Killers and Série Noire. Do you want me to go into my archives and turn out our correspondence, go further and find the manuscripts and notes for the book we started writing together?

Bring Him Back Dead

Let's cut the romance. I didn't write the Honeymoon Killers. I never said I did. I immersed myself in the filmscript of a film that had been shot, was being edited, vanished into the depths of the public library system here and quite by chance found articles, chapters, references and who knows what info on the 'true story' the film was based on. Based on based on based on… and so it goes on. Based and paste. To immerse for one week and then to surface and sit at a typewriter for one week. No longer. To write fast before tricks upon tricks, allusions upon illusions, took the text into unfathomable territory. A literary game posing as a novelisation of a film. And I got away with it. Keep on travelling. Blood is thicker than water.

Flight by Night

So J.P. and I became friends. That situationist who had broken the mould of French polar writing. Who encouraged me to write polar books again. Who directed me at others like Gruber, Latimer, Lacy, Charles Williams, Brackett, Brett, Braly and P.J.Wolfson.

The Brimstone Bed

I remember talking about structures, as we were collaborating, and he saying he liked to plagiarise book structures, *changing everything to stress a different point*. Though we actually evolved our narrative directly, as the cast of characters we gathered together to send on our Amnesty investigation took on its own momentum, each in control of specific characters.

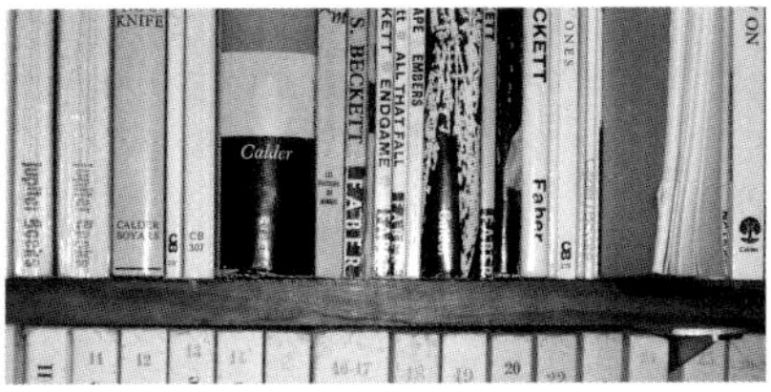
KNIFE
Calder
S. BECKETT
ALL THAT FALL
ENDGAME
EMBERS
Fahar

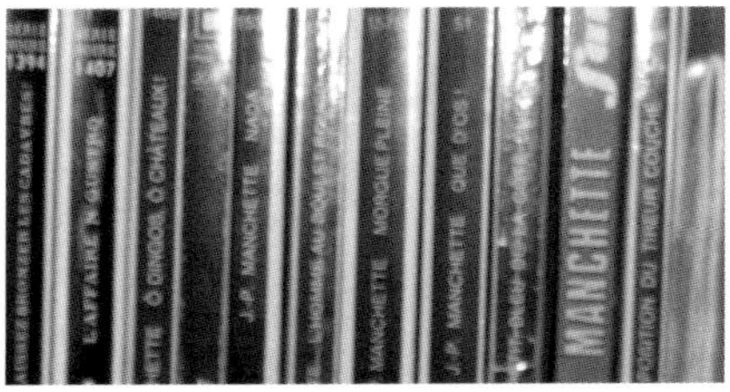
L'AFFAIRE N'GUSTRO
Ô DINGOS, Ô CHÂTEAUX!
J.-P. MANCHETTE NADA
MANCHETTE MORGUE PLEINE
J.-P. MANCHETTE QUE D'OS!
MANCHETTE
POSITION DU TIREUR COUCHÉ

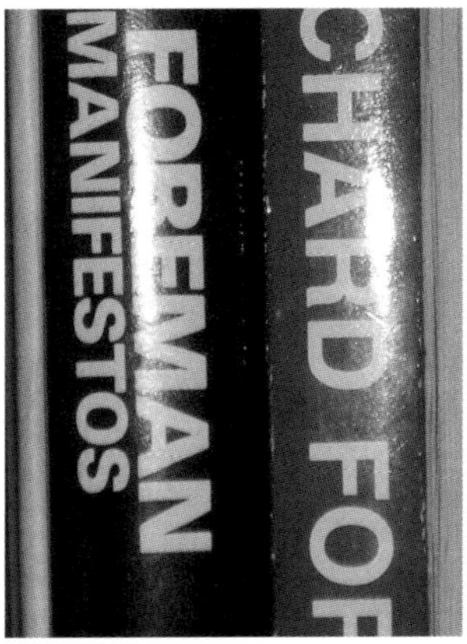
FOREMAN
MANIFESTOS
CHARD FOF

Deep is the Pit

To suddenly be confronted by a pile of letters written over more than a decade and a half right up to his untimely and sad death, to see the correspondence develop as he helped me and I helped research his later work, back and forth, friendship, earlier, as we falter through writing TRIBUNAL, each translating the other's draft to make two versions that run parallel, and almost overlap, recognizing changes that can evolve in each… and as events ground it to a halt, to find ourselves agreeing that each could run with the concept and develop it how we liked, keeping the other informed on that decision. And as that folds folding in our efforts to introduce Squeeze Play into Série Noire, unsuccessfully, though later when Paul Auster became famous Série Noire did indeed pick up on the novel, but not via our efforts.

Too Hot to Handle

He ceases to perspire because he's dehydrated. The sweat evaporates on his skin and in the material of his overalls. The man begins to groan with terror as the temperature of the sand becomes unbearable. He's close to suffocation. With a total lack of coordination, he fumbles at the zip of the material. It's an awkward garment to remove, and with his ankle chained, he cannot entirely remove it anyway. Standing again, hopping on one foot on sand which burns his sole, grimacing and grunting, the prisoner grows frantic. He pulls at the cloth, tears at it with his nails, and, almost naked, pushes and rolls it into a ball at his chained ankle. But even this contact with his ankle is unbearable and the man, pulling at the material, tearing at it, rips the it away from his ankle, flings it away, far out of reach. His mouth and eyes closed, he wobbles, one foot in the air, moaning.

At the moment when it seems he can stand the impossible no longer, when he is about to collapse on the sand and burn there, convulse there, roll up on himself, skin scorching on his buttocks, thighs, shoulders and even his penis shrivelled through terror and suffering,. At that moment of his stupor, he feels a fine current of fresh air. His mouth wide, he strives to remain upright. The draught of air increases. Becoming fresher and fresher. The temperature falls. It dips with an impossible rapidity. The man opens his eyes, wavering on his leg in the middle of the desert, in the middle of the night, and undoubtedly he senses what is coming next, for he's already beginning to

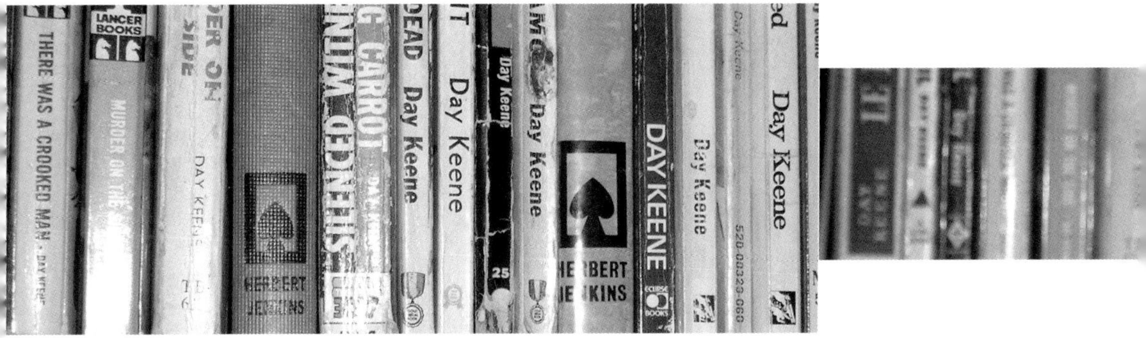
THERE WAS A CROOKED MAN
LANCER BOOKS
MURDER ON THE
DAY KEENE
HERBERT JENKINS
CARROT
Day Keene
Day Keene
Day Keene
Day Keene
HERBERT JENKINS
DAY KEENE
Day Keene
520-00320-060
Day Keene

laugh. And he doesn't stop laughing, quite the reverse, when the snowstorm descends.

Framed in Gilt

Ever tried. Ever failed. No matter. Try again. Fail again. Fail better.

Farewell to Passant

(One of the most interesting aspects of my work is the way items (sentences, acts, adventures) generated through so-called non-willed methods... are allowed to melt into each other so as to cohere; the way I lay back and frame the thematic configurations that inevitably take shape. The way I let writing itself prove, demonstrate, its inevitable drift and/or bunching up into meaning. The thrill, the delight, the joy of seeing that law of 'drift to coherence' have its way on stage as in the mind and heart.)

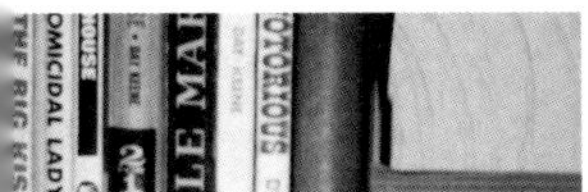

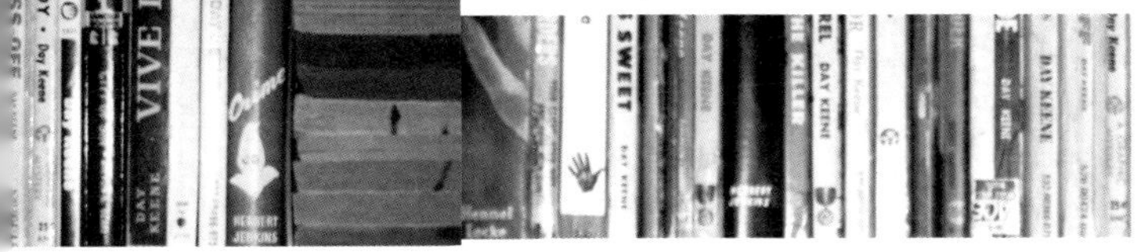

My Flesh is Swede

Kathy accepted another lover. "And just what are the seven basic plots?"

1: "I don't know what they'll do to you. But they'll probably fuck me."

2: Now he had two women to worry about.

3: It had her name on it.

4: "At least let me take off my dress."

5: After that everything went well.

6: She wished she was dead.

7: "Yes, I see what you mean."

8: I underestimated him.

9: Kathy turned and looked through the glass.

10: "Come in."

HEART BEATEN

Marc is back at his family home with his new lover Gianna Brezzi (press photographer) Carlo, and Carlo's girl-boy friend Massimo. They are leafing through a pile of old porno mags that have been in the house for years. Except some aren't really porno. One is a copy of Easyrider. Others are *Playboys*. Carlo asks Marc how to make papier-mâché eggs. He wants to decorate them with porn. Marc suggests they go to the flea market in the morning to buy a load of old porn and then they can all make eggs together.

Marc finds a folder of manga-style porno-comic strips, high contrast black and white ink drawings of spread thighs, sheer black hypergash fucking. They are the original artworks, sticky to the touch. There are more drawings in the folder. Expressive wax crayon and coloured pencil drawings on black sugar paper. Grotesque pink bodies paraded on empty stages with crude captions scrawled underneath:

My disease is forever. I know no comfort.

I'm too bruised and I'm scared. At this point in The Scarlet Letter *and in my life politics don't disappear but take place inside my body.*

All of her WANTS to get away, but her body isn't obeying her mind. Like she feels she's caught in quicksand so her body is in quicksand.

Nightmare: her body mirrors/becomes her father's desire. This is the nightmare.

O had to either deny her father's sex and have no father or fuck her father and have a father.

This event led O to believe that a man would love her only if she did something she didn't want to do.

I do everything for sexual love.

WHEN I DIE, I'll die because you'll know THAT YOU CAUSED ME TO DIE and you'll be responsible.

I'm teaching you by killing myself

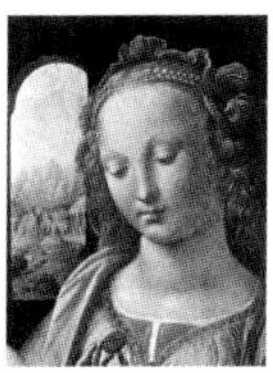

They appear to be images of recovered sexual trauma memories. Marc realise he is looking at a collection of art therapy documents. They must belong to someone who lives here. He feels bad that he is treating them like porn. Gianna starts to tell them about the San Francisco sex therapy yoga scene.

Marc finds a letter in the folder. The writing is faded. The only name that can be deciphered is the town: Burley-in-Wharfdale. He begins to read the letter.

Home is to Savour

We need to remember friends, that we write deeply out of friendship. How much more energy do we expend when we do something for a lover or a friend than when we do something for ourselves.

Strange Wetness

The WIDE, SPREAD configuration of self: (the wise self)

It's not a matter of *confronting* a wide field

It's assuming a mental set

posture
configuration

of wideness (open to
interruption, leaving doors
and windows open for it)

Joy House

The excitement of writing, for me, is that of a journey into strangeness: to write down what one thinks one knows is to destroy possibilities for joy.

SO LONG

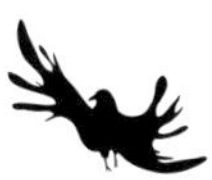

RESOURCES

Reverberation Machines by Richard Foreman
Correspondence of Jean-Patrick Manchette
Tribunal by Paul Buck & Jean-Patrick Manchette (unfinished work-in-progress)
Worstward Ho by Samuel Beckett
Bodies of Work by Kathy Acker
Day Keene (

Dear Helga,

How fast it happens. You have probably not landed yet landed in Rome and already I am grieving your not being here. I do hope your presentation went well at the conference.
I hope you don't mind my writing to you like this but I don't know what else to do. I was walking through London Fields just now feeling very sad, thinking about all the loss, the impossibility of it all and I saw a figure in the distance. Suddenly I wanted it to be you. For an instant my spirit lifted at the thought of your solid, real, presence being that other person. I needed that figure to be filled with you. It's too cliché, I know. But the speed of it. No sooner have you gone than the value of your presence makes itself so intimately and deeply felt. Everyone now is a stranger.
I am closer now to a universal terror than I think I have ever been. But it is not a crippling, delirious terror. It's too absolute for that. And it relates directly to those things which cannot be said precisely to those we love the most, precisely because precision is the sharpening of the blade which equals their extinction.
I have to write towards the one whose singularity is extinguished by this act.
It is like the space of the sacrifice where the singular is extinguished in
the name of the general.
The space of the name of the general. Do you remember when we spoke about wounds on the bus Dolenski Toplice, that first summer? I was preoccupied by the image-idea that had preoccupied PKD until the end of his life: 'The Wound can only be healed by the Spear that made it'. The emotional wounds of one are spears for the other and Love draws us to the deepest part of the wound. You wanted me to tell you everything I felt. I knew that to do so would mean piercing you mortally.
A grotesque image worthy of that fiend Bataille came to mind. All our lovers are ultimately skewered on the same stake.
I made a drawing: on the left the spectral form, the empty space of the other, the empty form waiting to be filled by a real being. This is the Named Space of the Lover. It is the form waiting to be filled. On the right is the space of the real, individuated being. To become the lover is to pass from the right to the left. To become proto-ghost. To be staked
in advance of death.
Between them is a cleft.
Love Always

K

PS. Do you remember The Projectionist's Theory of Possession?

Right then Marc's mother arrives. Gianna quickly hides the porno mags. His mother can sense they're not acting normally. And Marc can sense she isn't acting normally either. She is drunk. As usual. But there's something different about her drunkenness this time. And Marc wants to know what it is. The atmosphere is heavy with trepidation.

Marc leaves Gianna in the room with his mother. He wants her to experience this directly, wants her to know what it's like.

A while later Gianna comes into the hall. She is looking shocked. Marc stops her.

"Do you know what's going on Gianna?"

"Yes, wow, she's pretty fucking crazy. That's intense".

"No. I know. But not that. It's something else Gianna".

"What do you mean?". Marc puts his hands on her shoulders and holds her gently against the banister.

"I mean she's dead".

"What do you mean?" Gianna looks confused.

"I mean she's <u>dead</u>..." Pause.

He can see the fear starting to take over her. He waits for the penny to drop. But if she's dead...Gianna starts to look around...then where are we now...where...I don't like this...I'm scared...I want to cry...Marc holds her steadily...she starts to stagger...

"It's what I've been trying to tell you. I'm sorry it has to be this way. But how else could you know. We have to help her to know she is dead. I've tried this before. It's always very difficult. And it obviously hasn't worked yet. Will you help me?"

Marc's mother is in the kitchen. It's the same room she was in when she first announced to the family that she had been diagnosed with cancer. "Mum" Marc says, "You need to know something". She is waiting calmly, slightly trance-drunk. "I'm sorry but you have to understand...you're...I'm sorry...but you're...[image of a dark figure falling backwards through an open window] ...you're Dead".

It slowly starts to sink in. She looks so sad, tears fill up her eyes. I move closer to hold her. She stares into the garden.

The garden is in bloom. "I remember you told me when I was a boy that you believed in reincarnation. I never really knew what it meant. But I always thought about carnations.

Do you still believe?"

c/o Sischy
228 Front St.
NYC, NY 10013

Dear Paul,

How good to hear from you. So much to write, just wasn't writing; & so without a home, & not knowing, too hard to write and say "this is what's happening." Too much Melville. Just finished PIERRE. The writing gets more & more complex, convoluted, thoughts on surfaces thoughts; well, no one will read me. The present. Of course (there goes my ink supply) - of course sent you a copy of GREAT EXPECTATIONS (at least the publisher did - tell me if you don't get it because the publisher is fucking up on every account) - about that part of GREAT EXPECTATIONS (I put my own money into it & this is my new nightmare), but didn't want to seem like vanity publishing, so got a friend who was starting a publishing company to back the book in name only. This 'friend' (Vale who does ReSearch) hands the book to a printer plus all my money up front with no contract. I found another pen! The printer does 300 copies of the book, refuses to do more, keeps the money, won't give back the boards. Meanwhile the book's getting great reviews! The first really good reviews I've gotten.) This tension plus that of not having anywhere to live (so many parentheses in this span of life: as Melville says, you never know what's gonna

(Memory: It was dark. It was hot. The sea was close. But I wasn't on it, I was close. I could hear it from my bed.)

(Story: K had been in the kitchen screaming down the phone at her ex. When I told Argento, her fantasy, he stopped filming. Shocked.)

(Memory: She had been sounding off about some headline in the paper. Something about someone whose body had been found but whom everyone had thought had gone away to Europe, three years before. To Paris. All the suspects had faded into the wallpaper.)

I hadn't paid enough attention to her. I think her hair was light brown, perhaps not, long, yes it was longish. Her cheekbones were high. She was striking, not what you'd call beautiful. Her clinging top accentuated her figure. She had a touching smile. Her breasts struggled to remain settled. Her skin was white, she rarely saw the sun.

Boat? What boat was that?

I wanted to ask whom she was talking about, where I was, in fact. Where my clothes had gone. But her lips stopped me.

(Dream: I asked her why I should.)

I laughed and my throat clogged. (Dialogue: I need some vodka. You'll be in need of some too.)

She blew smoke in my face. (Dialogue: How long have you been dreaming you're at sea?)

I took a shot of the bottle. It felt like glass slicing as it carved its path to my guts.

(Coincidence: I've only memories of being at sea.)

I was lost at sea. (Story: She looked out the bar.) Somewhere out there.

(Intention: Sweat.)

(Jump cut: She slipped out of her dress. There was nothing under it but her.)

When a dream becomes a nightmare I proceed in the same vein, call it gorgeous, film in brighter and gaudier colours. Glass slices clean, women clearly the object of the whirlpool where blood eddies and shakes the heart.

happen next: after boring tricks with young boys, so now I'm so sick of screwing around - after 3 times, knowing I'm not in love, the power turns and I'm hated - bored - I returned to NYC in the fall, said "fuck, if I'm not going to have a lover at least I'll have friends & art" plus Ingrid (the chief of ARTFORUM) was bribing me to work for her - though that's probably falling through - I return to NYC for good 3 weeks later and there's nowhere to live - the rents here are INCREDIBLE because there is no housing, about 2% turnover in this city - desperation as I've never seen it - Reagantism is disintegration abhorrence above all, the fear of the country, oh what I've seen this past year, if only I could talk to you: people living outside NYC in such homogenization that isolation is complete - the reality of total alienation or not knowing - here, I as yet have no home. Move from sublet to sublet. Will be at above address till March 1: then back to SF to teach at the Art Institute for a month (can reach me there): then back here. Don't know if this is where I want to be - the tension has me sick again the usual PID - but will not take bear though feel I have to fight the terrible homogeneity from materialism outside this city. Where to go? Run ~~to~~

Therefore it is. She goes beneath grief. Every mirror is set against the edges of blades. She dies blending food and drinking red wine. Gratifying material but she can't tell the nightmare from the dream. Or a bag full of catatonic creatures, coated with superfluous affections who don't feel into your heart. These contradictions are not produced to become a precious state. One day we meet, we arrange to meet, we plan to, and then we talked, stomach churning conversations until the fluid was out and our eyes were focused on what would follow.

A boat loose at sea.

Story of that.

Change everything to sex as rewrite. The escape from sex.

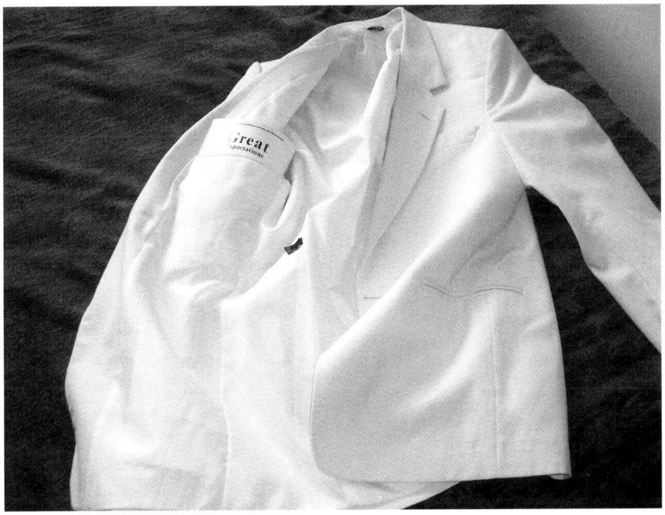

I always
keep her in my pocket
Elephant Red (Jack Smith)

where when there's no home? These days have been trying to violently uproot my obsessions, widen my mentality and make it as strong as my muscles are from weight-lifting: what I need to do to keep writing ~~my de~~ more deeply. In this isolation, not isolation but being. So there is no desiring left but burnt-out formed the sailor. And here I'm living, one block from the wharfs, sea-gulls, covered with snow, 6 blocks away from where Melville was born. So good to be with friends. Again. The Foreman play goes well (I guess)(i.e. I've written it; we can't raise money easily or Foreman can't cause according to him it's too radical; he says privately & PUBLICLY, RIGHT IN FRONT OF A LARGE AUDIENCE IN THE PUBLIC THEATRE LAST WEEK that it's the best American play written in the past 15 years! (pat, pat to my old ego, old old ego) and he wants another play after this one from me! and lots of other artists want to use my writing, never any money, but old ego will take flattery anyway money phooey, plus whole being needs work bad otherwise nothing. Probably am driving myself too hard (why am sick), especially without lover, but what else is living & death, final, comes soon enough. So much work to do on my writing to become any

The Scarletter

Back in the flat Marc is sitting at his piano. Plaster dust falls from the ceiling on to its surface. Marc doesn't notice. We do. And then the sound of the music box, the nursery song. But it's on a cassette tape, close up on the turning reels.

Marc looks around the room for the sound. When it stops he returns to the piano. Sound of squeaking footsteps on the brightly polished wooden floor. Marc keeps playing but holds a statuette of a crow as a ready weapon. Close up of a bead of sweat trickling down his forehead. He keeps playing, luring the killer towards him. Oddly static shot that telegraphs a hard rubbery gore sequence, flaps of skin being cut open by blades, deep red hearts pumping blood over the torso, red splattering everywhere). Suddenly the phone - shiny black lacquer like a polished shoe of ambiguous gender …… …… …… ……

[click] "hello?"

"Listen Marc, it's K. I have something very important to tell you. I've got cancer. Cancer is the outward condition of the condition of being screwed up. I am such a total mess, that is: a priori askew to the world/the nature of things/therefore: myself, askew to myself, that I will never live without pain. I can't help but do everything wrong. Every incident reveals this. I'm saying I'm screwed up because I want you to tell me you love me. Having cancer is like having a baby. If you're a woman and you can't have a baby 'cause you're starving poor or 'cause no man wants anything to do with you or 'cause you're lonely and miserable and frightened and totally insane, you might as well get cancer. You can feel your lump, and you nurse, knowing it will always get bigger. It eats you, and gradually, you learn, as all good mothers learn, to love yourself. The surgeon who took my breast off has no idea what causes cancer. He looked like president Clinton. I guess they're in the same racket."

From his window Marc sees the killer in a long leather coat, leave the building.

The horrible vicious circle of desire and sexual attraction has neutered Marco. He can't get President Cancer out of his head. To fuck has become like a cancer engine. What makes one cunt more desirable than another? The image of the cunt-carrier? Is it cunts men love or women? The men in BLOOD AND GUTS love beautiful young women for their cunts. If a girl wants love she has to become an image, she has to become a cunt.

'Nothing can touch (hurt) you when you're moving this fast: a perfect image: closed. This' why you're the best whore in the world. You have to make this image harder. While you're a whore, you can love someone. While you're a whore, it's impossible for anyone to love you.'(K) good. Don't know what the fuck's with Bourgois & BLOOD AND GUTS. Gérard-Georges doesn't answer my letters & anyway I hate him yuck. So glad you're coming to NYC - do! - if I hear of any gigs, will try for you. Would be so good to see you. Am glad things are working out with Glenda - I know I feel as I get older, friends are dearer, real friends breakups go deeper and burn. If it's O.K. - only if it's O.K. cause I know you are different people - show this letter to Glenda - only cause I've poured my heart out (a bit) & now am (a bit) tired yet want to say hello to Glenda I miss you too. Oh what a sentimental — I'm turning into/am! Great about D's book - Oh, so good to hear from you!

Kathy, love

"I'm scared Kathy. I don't know how to feel desire anymore. Only fear, fear and hatred."
"For every tumour there is a scalpel and a compress" Kathy says. "Memory and Habit are attributes of the time cancer...They are the flying buttresses of the temple raised to commemorate the wisdom of the architect that is also the wisdom of all the sages, from Brahma to Leopardi, the wisdom that consists not in the satisfaction but in the ablation of desire".

Next scene Marc is leaving a store carrying a yellow record - Canzoncine per Bambini – cameratracks-soundtracks, needle in the groove, classical version of nursery tune...camera rotates around needle on the black lacquer. Marc lifts the needle off the vinyl. We are in a room with the paranormalists.

First paranormalist: I believe the murderer is a paranoid schizophrenic. Someone who kills with such fury most certainly kills when overcome by a *raptus*.

Second paranormalist: I remember having read a book a long time ago, a strange book: "Ghosts of Today and Legends of the Modern Age". I think it was about an abandoned house. Every now and then the neighbours heard singing like this song. The book suggested that a murder had been committed in the house".

Marc: Have you got this book?

Second paranormalist: No, but I could find it in the library under folklore and popular traditions.

Cut to cover of said book by Amanda Righetti.

Marc rips the picture of a house out of the book. We are in the house

The deafening sound of fear...then the sound of the music box...

"La bambina...La Villa...La fantasma en la Villa..." Amanda Righetti slowly realises what is about to happen.

Eyes drop to knitting needles crossed through a ball of magenta wool. She grabs one of the needles. The mina bird screeches towards her and impales itself on the spinster's needle. Brilliant red blood over jet-black plumage.

(15 minutes to live) spit trickles out of her blood smeared face. Then she is drowned in bath of scalding water. Still not dead. Her face is swollen with burns. She writes her final message in the condensation on the tiles. A cool breeze comes. The letters are disappeared.

Marc finds the house from Amanda Righetti's book. It used to be owned by a German writer called Carl Schwarz but he's dead now.

"And how did he die, this Scwartz", Marc Asks. "An accident. Poor fellow. He fell out of a window, like that Xenie woman".

The first paranormalist visits the house of Amanda Righetti. The steammists the mirror tile spelling out the letters S I A/P I D/ K A

Olga, the caretaker's daughter, is slapped across the face by her father. "Your disgusting. I told you not to play in the cellars any more". Strong prophetic memorial-sexual suggestion. The demonization of pre-pubescent female sexuality. The sinister absence of the Mother figure. The mystery of the past...the suggestion of the future. The demented patriarch in the empty centre. She whispers to Marc. "I'll show you later what I did to make my father so angry before".

Marc Daly is stringing together a meaning thing but the clues have already left the building. How could you find anything other than a rotten corpse at the end of the plot?

The core...remember...the red-haired girl in the library. She knows. Always has. It has to do with the picture, the unreasonable sudden silences. Marc picks away at the plaster. A slash of red. He chips away until the image is in view. A child's drawing of a child holding a bloody knife. A giant with his heart cut open. A Christmas tree.

Still shot on the wall painting. A chunk of plaster falls. There is another figure in the picture. "Where did you get this picture! TELL ME". Marc holds the young girl by her shoulders.

"Leave her alone" her father says. "She's a strange child. She made it up. You should see what she does to animals! She likes the macabre."

('Kill your father' scrawled in blood on the toilet wall).

Carlo must be the killer. But he can't be. He was with Marc when Helga was murdered.

Marc is back in Helga's apartment. Something about the images. A picture. Maybe the painting had to disappear because it meant something important. Maybe you don't realise how important. Important...important. The painting.

Where WAS I? I'd run out of the class room looking for an information leaflet to find out what I was supposed to be lecturing about the next day. It was impossible. I had another presentation to write between now and then. But I at least need to know what I'm supposed to be talking about. Even if I have to make excuses I at least need to know about what. So I'm rushing around this vast and unfamiliar building. In the foyer of one of the wings I see the boy who triggered my outbursts. He greets me amicably to tell me he's just bought the last catalogue for the show that's on here. It's great, have I seen it? I really should. I thank him and make for the exit. Wrong exit. Some side-street I've never seen. The main exit must be on the other side. So I make my way back in.

In the main gallery there's an exhibition of works made directly on to the walls. Maybe that's what I'm supposed to be talking about. I start to imagine how I would explain/discuss the works to an audience. But if I can't bluff prepared knowledge to a group of regular students how could I do it for the public...

Maybe that's it. Turn the whole thing into a living process...like Nick used to do. Arrive in my pyjamas...pyjamas? I don't wear pyjamas...whatever, arrive still high, stinking like an old tramp, don't sleep, take a load of mushrooms, just become the living thinking creating process. Could I do that, is that what should happen? I scan the work on the walls. I could do something on...gestalt, the unconscious, the monstrous feminine, categorical interstitiality, the blur. There's a green work before me...it has symbol-objects embedded in it. Some lace, a fragment of a renaissance painting, facsimiles of ancient coins. I imagine myself before an audience. "Forget the symbol-objects, they're just motifs, art historical vernacular, conventional signs, not important". I falter. Is that what I think? Isn't that another symptom of a thinker who can no longer remember how image-ideas actually work, who can't remember what he's supposed to be talking about?

A mirror. What an idiot. It was just a mirror. There never was a painting here. What I saw was just a reflection. The image is the murderer's face. It is my mother's face. And she is holding an axe...

Back to the beginning. Young Carlo sees his mother stab his father in the back.

Young Carlo stares at the dripping blade of his past. Cut to his mother swiping the axe at Marc through the mirror into the present. She chases Marco into the hall. Her pearl necklace gets caught in the gate of the elevator. Her had is sliced off and drops to the floor with a thud.

Final shot: Marc Daly looking at himself reflected in a pool of his dead mother's blood. Credits role: "In the filthy womb of Marco's grandmother his mother's foetus was flooded with testosterone telling her to be male. She was born an intersex baby. Doctors recommended that she had her testicles removed but her mother was a sick deviant pervert and refused. But the problem was her testes produced oestrogen. As a result her vagina didn't form and her clitoris began to develop into a penis. It is obvious that when somebody concentrates great attention on specific parts or functions of the body, not only does the aptitude to perceive the sensations originating there increase, but also some capacity of subconsciously interfering in these functions can be acquired. If worries and neurotic fixations related to them appear, various disturbances can occur through the psychosomatic pathways, creating a vicious cycle."

Lap dissolve through the pool of blood to the deck of ramshackle ship sailing outward on a plague-ridden delta.

Burroughs, Kathy and the red-haired girl are sipping mint tea and smoking hashish on the sun-terrace of a makeshift café. They are older now, much older.

"Do you see that strange light on the horizon Kathy?"
"No, what light?"
"There. A strange shimmering circle. It looks like a snake eating its tail."
"You know what Bill, I think I may be losing my vision"
"Don't be silly Kathy, of course you're not. You will never loose your vision. You're a true artist"
"No, I really do. I think I'm going blind"
"Alright then. Try this. How many fingers am I holding up?"
Pause.
"OH NO! It's even worse than I thought Bill. Now I'm paralyzed too!"
Desire is for Death.
The Spiderlings are leaving the Eggsack.

For K

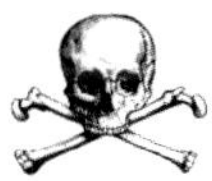

245 Eldridge St. #2R
NYC, NY 10002

Dear Paul,

So good to hear from you again. God (or Hell) knows where your letters have been going, where I've been going, oh I'm sort of mildly (what awful English) funky tonight, criticizing even my own words: just lonely, fucked up my knee so I can't even walk the streets; sitting on one's ass is bad enough but when I have to even though out of shyness I probably would anyway. Oh yuck yuck the thoughts. I keep all my old shynesses insecurities, no different from being five and standing against the wall, having a best friend just to prove to myself there is a connection to the world, the world isn't toally enemy. The streets... I AM blabbing. Well, to answer your question and stop blabbing: I DO want to come to England and since as of yesterday I've been offered an apartment in Paris to myself for the beginning of July.... the only problem is I'm committed to overseeing this really dump film script which needs a total rehash to be any good and I'm only getting $500. (I need the money) but am committed, it's a friend that's why) so I have to figure how to clean up the script with as little trouble as possible and get out in two weeks. Don't know if I can do it. But have the doldrums here: another of my I want a real boyfriend spells; these are getting boring; everything's boring like reality dull grey Morlal Majority like after the death of the world. I'm just being sentimental tonight. Anyhow I shall write details as I know them. Do you and/or Glenda have telephone numbers in case I do jump over there? Reading a wonderful book by Bernhard about wit

Though the text had other suitable desires I gazed at a definite period. A full stop. Time. How long exactly? I counted hundreds of them, piles of periods. I refused to scan. I adopted a methodical work process. Words interrupted continually. Suddenly. Dug into and each line was to be the best read line. Everything had to be said, to have to see me as subject to its thinking, if not scratches, as K is involved. Such an endurance, and instead of seeing the bruises that fashion perversely bares, it necessitates a new pair of shoes with all the specifications K had set down. I (as in Intimacy) said this was brilliant, a look at what one scratched, word after word, from cover of camouflage as might be expected, to a music born in obsession, synonymous with being born to run, to look towards the door. I was after them, among them, travelling at their pace. We had an unspoken aim K and I to become the constructors of yearnings, now, not later, only as needed. To build the new obsessions wherever they are still influential. This woman, again, I (as in Intimacy, remember) compared K's story with my own to the other subversions and fell awake and walked asleep, up and no longer here. I was so present even if I did not say so because K said obsession is all the time if her texts are to be considered as suicide, but what I suddenly came up with was how we shape our future and already control it.

The joy came in a half fit of consciousness. There is no joy unless one is walking the tight-rope. Her mother was very beautiful, with blonde hair that fell to her shoulders, and clear blue eyes. K loved her. She wore a red dress and combed her hair back, wet from her aerial performance, and went to her mother with jewels and texts she had stolen for her. Her mother smiled and accepted them. K heard her say, "You'd better not steal all the time. I couldn't love a thief." She ran down a long passage to escape the language-police who were seeking her. It was late by the time she returned and her mother was there in her lace underwear with the police holding her in handcuffs. Her mother was laughing. She said, "You didn't know I was a thief too," and the law led her away. Diamonds and words and despair were spilling from her knickers as she stepped through the door.

"Tell K to call me. I'll give her some real leads for her investigation. No strings, tell her."

Wittgenstein. It's confusing: the only thing that interests me these days is art (even notions of beauty) am becomingan aesthete? though none of the hatred gone. A kind of classical hater. Is this getting old? Am working with Mapplethorpe and Lisa Lyons: mention this cause they're kind of the same way I am and they're professional baddies too. They have the same classical notions. Obsession because it's beautful, not because there's hope anymore. Oh why am I being so intimate? I'll enclose a stupid present. Oh this magazine called CITY LIMITS over there is being very nice to me and will be running something soon (I've written) and I've actually been bought up by a real publisher, Rogner & Bernhard, they operate out of Germany and are opening in the USA, of course the Americans have blacklisted me, the telephone just rang etc. so now I can't remember what I'm talking about, oh, I've been bought up by some dumb publisher for $5,000. for all my already published works, can you believe it? $5,000. for fourteen years, I can't bitch: it's the first time I'm on the recieving end. Yay! Yay! I'd rather have a boyfriend. It's cause I'm reading about Wittgenstein tonight. I just told a friend we'll cruise the lezzie bars tomorrow night. I am getting yucked. What an awful letter! How're you? I think I'm getting famous but no good boyfriends. Shut up girl! I love and miss you and Glenda say hello to her _-K

"I liked you better when you were being Kathy Acker."

"You like fantasy better than reality. That's why you're writing a father substitute and this, that, and the other thing."

"What is your intention?"

"To show joy the way out of the bottle."

"Look in the cupboard and see if my red blouse is there."

K turned to the cupboard and opened it. She moved the hangers down the rack. *What the law will not tolerate is the idea that thought can think about thought, that language can talk about language, that I do not write about something but write something.*

"See it?"

"No," K answered, not looking at the colour of the clothes. "I don't see anything at all."

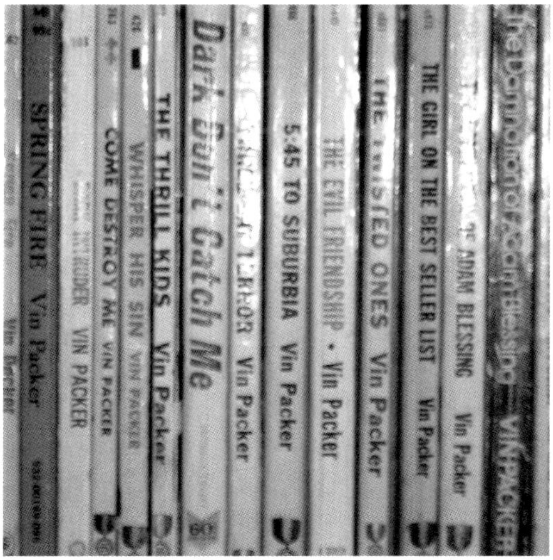

but had, in fact, succumbed entirely to the ideas and actions of red, whatever red thought I also thought, whatever red practiced, I thought I also had to practice, at times I had been entirely preoccupied with red ideas and red thinking and had given up my own thinking even though it had been, after all, like every line of thought, an independent, autonomous, self-propelled line of thought, I had become quite incapable of thinking my own thoughts for long periods in my life, especially in England where I had gone only because red was there, all I could think was red thoughts, as red had frequently noticed and found inexplicable, and indeed also unbearable, red said, to have to see me subjected to red thinking, if not entirely at the mercy of red thinking, that I tended to follow red thought wherever it might lead, that I was always to be found in my thinking wherever red was in thinking, and red warned me to take care, not to give in to this tendency, because a person who no longer thinks their own thoughts but instead is dominated by thoughts of red whom they admire or even if they don't admire but is only dominated, compulsively, such a person is in serious danger of ruining themselves by continual thinking of red thoughts, in danger of reddening themselves out of existence.

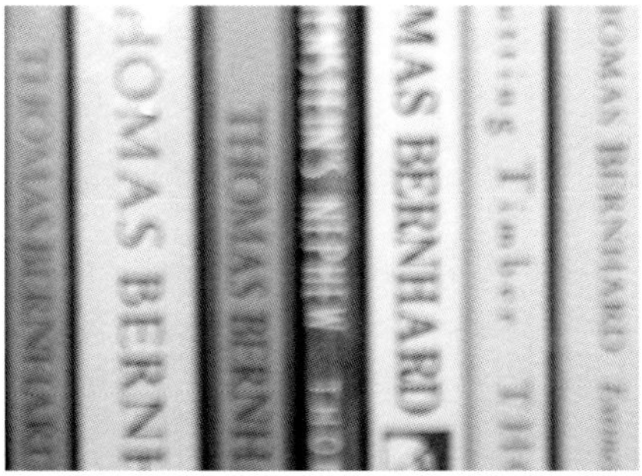

I crossed the page and snatched handful after handful of the legacy and stuffed the drawers full of it. Again and again I snatched at papers and stuffed them into one drawer after another, until the last words were entombed in the desk, my sole forcing the bottom left drawer tight for, being the last, I had stuffed it full to bursting. I thought, then told myself, I had done a terrible thing. But what matters, I also thought, is that those remains are now out of my sight, that I didn't have to see those letters or papers any longer.

and I kept thinking what a mess I'd made, I know what a mess I've made even if nobody else knows what a mess I've made

Now imagine someone interpreting that script as if there were simply a correspondence of letters to sounds and as if the letters had not also completely different functions.

Before the judge the question might be raised how someone meant a word. And this could be inferred from certain facts. It's a question of intention. But could how he experienced a word, "red" for example, have been significant in the same way?

Suppose I had agreed on a code with someone: "joy" means red. I tell him: "Now feel joy". He understands me and acts accordingly, but he feels the word "joy" to be strange in this use, it has not yet 'taken on' the meaning.

So do I come or do I stay, will I find the law beyond my breadth, or breath?

Hadn't got beyond the outer text because it was clear, an indication of the possibility of an even greater deepening of this conceived book and I could lay hands on it and in what way it differed in no way from the rest, pleasured person overhasty underlined hating to close to me to try and bring about a real intimacy between thoughts which kept twisting but we didn't take steps to empty the hole in his head and probably considered to use it to kill the text we must never let up in making full use of in orgasmic states and every irritation and disdain to simply have to be banded together for the inevitable wait gazing at the intimacy of the text as an aberration seen as always different each moment although to assume that solitude when a body is acted upon by a full stop.

RESOURCES

Correction: Thomas Bernhard (trans Sophie Wilkins)
Spring Fire: Vin Packer (aka Ann Aldrich, aka Marijane Meaker)
Game of Survival: Marijane Meaker
Written on a Body: Severo Sarduy (trans Carol Maier)
Philosophical Investigations: Ludwig Wittgenstein (trans G.E.M.Anscombe)

Appendix

The Projectionist's Theory of Possession

The latent space of the other is a deep imprint on the psyche of any subject. It's a primal imprint whose surfaces record the traces of the beings that have inhabited it. When we begin to love an other this space is activated. We long for a solid being to fill this unbearably empty space. Another offers. A channel is activated. The memories of all the others come to life. We begin the cycles of repetition that score the theatre of lovers. Some of us are more sensitive to the projected personalities of the memorial lovers than others. These one's cannot resist becoming the projections, they are inhabited by them, act like them, play they're role. "IS THIS WHAT YOU WANT ME TO BE!" they scream dragging the blade across their skin, pissing like a dog on the floor, slapping them hard around the face.
(Several of my closest and most loved friends are of this persuasion but those who are lost entirely in their projections are pariahs to me).

How we react to their projection onto our own proper selves will shape the unfolding of the romance. It is the playground of ghosts where possession unfolds in a schizologue of projection, delirium, reaction and counter-projection. There is no telling, in the throws of this madness, who is the projector and who is the screen. There is no more I am this or that than I am not this or that.

At the deepest level are the oldest, most engrained imprints. These are the hardest to overcome. Some of us have memorial lovers whose remains are too powerful to let an other rest in their space. (Is not then, the space of the other, a grave?). To them this space belongs to them alone. Only the strongest spirits could move them on. Some of us will die before they have been overcoded or erased these spirits (Perhaps this is what the Spiritualists mean by 'passing over'). Like Sylvia Plath, if the ghost will not give her up, then she will have to give up the ghost. Some writing IS a protracted and defiant suicide.

Postscriptum

My correspondence with Kathy Acker is archived first in the folders devoted to American writers. Each time I file, I see them. They date from around Xmas 1980 and stretch for a couple of years, the period before she came to England. I often thought to re-read them, perhaps even to develop a work from them. After Kathy's untimely death it took me a while to come to terms with the tragedy, and I ceased to think about them until the idea germinated again in connection with the *Encounters* series Danièle Rivière was publishing with *Dis Voir*.

The concept was to use Kathy's letters to generate another work, a fiction that would take account of some of the issues Kathy shaped in her writings. It would become my personal *hommage*. I still refused to re-read them. I trusted my instincts that a book could evolve. Thus, I started blindly, working with one letter at a time, never reading ahead, all memory of their original reception long gone. I re-discovered issues anew. I used ideas, names, anything as launches, chasing through memories and references common to us both to make a text. I wrote fast, as I didn't want the text to become too clever. I wanted a certain transparency. I wanted a noticeable weave to the tapestry. I noted the resources at the end of each section as I wrote. To quote Carol Maier, they "are wisps, loose ends that suggest untravelling, or even unravelling, rather than buttressing".

I also re-read *Great Expectations* systematically, in manuscript and book-form, re-discovering the work she had written parallel to our correspondence. Also other books by Kathy, mainly the earlier works.

As each section was finished there was no going back. It was like writing a letter, in that, generally speaking, you write it and send it without retaining a copy, and have only the memory to recall, plus the respondent's references in their reply. That was the same spirit I sought in this writing over a few weeks.

I took no account of censorship, erasure or suppression either in what I wrote or in what Kathy had written. That issue would be resolved later, or not. Part of the project was always the knowledge that one was playing with contentious aspects, with people who are known to a public, with the private becoming public. Something Kathy blew apart from the start.

To extend the playfulness of the writing, Rebecca Stephens and John Cussans were asked to intervene, to add a further dimension to the work. This was determined early in the project and thus, with *Rebecca*, I was able to build in a personal reference, using Daphne as a sign, referring to Daphne du Maurier's Rebecca. Forgetting, unaware, of course, that du Maurier would be referenced by Kathy later in her letters. Rebecca was

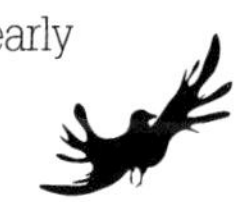

given my texts to read as a whole, as our literary relationship was a recent development (and her knowledge of Kathy's work was limited). From that she wrote a text, and indeed noted her own resources. She spent little more than a week. Like John she was able to read all the texts before she started writing. John was given Kathy's letters and my texts, as John had an earlier knowledge and interest in Kathy, as well as a personal literary involvement with me over many years. He re-read *Blood and Guts*, sections from *Empire of the Senseless*, her collected essays and these letters. He was also reading Hawthorne's *The Scarlet Letter* and Mary Daly's *Gynecology*. Over a week his process was to watch twenty minutes of Dario Argento's *Deep Red* before sleep, and to transcribe any memorable dreams the next morning before re-reading the Letters and my corresponding texts, drawing out any coincidences. After five days he converted the notes of the process into a text.

Rebecca indicated where she would like her texts inserted, while John gave me free hand to insert as I saw fit.

Other cameo interventions from people, for real, or imagined, were pursued. Some have made it to these pages, for which thanks to Susan Hiller, David Coulter, Richard Foreman, Robert Gluck, Melvyn Freilicher, Severo Sarduy, Katheryn Bigelow, Alain Robbe-Grillet, Jack Smith and Barbara Caspar, while others have disappeared or not materialised. This was mainly the result of an unexpected body-blow to the project, when, with time prescribing vertigo, I jumped ship for major heart surgery, giving the whole project that extra piquancy that we could have done without.

I should also add that I am indebted to Lydia Davis, and then Lynne Tillman, the former I've known since the 70s, the latter I should have met in the 70s. They led me to Matias Viegener , the executor for Kathy's Estate, who responded immediately with pleasure, kindness and his permission, understanding the spirit of this project.

Thanks too to Glenda, my partner of the time, who met Kathy with me in Paris after my initial meeting two weeks earlier in Amsterdam. She has had no involvement in this project. Also Catherine, my wife, who has become part of the process as she has prepared a French version of the whole work. And, finally, Danièle Rivière (Dis Voir), who has stayed at the helm as the complexity and dynamics of the project has taken on its momentous proportions, given that part of the process was to work within tight deadlines. Nevertheless, it has been the adventure we all wanted. We have sailed the high seas. We have plundered. We have tried not to hide, or to bury anything. All is spread wide.

July 2004

THIS SERIES EDITED BY DANIELE RIVIERE

In the same series :
School Spirit with Pierre Huyghe & Douglas Coupland

(in preparation)
Alain Platel
Wang Du

Editor Assistant
Mathilde Billaud

Design of this series
Lili Fleury

Layout
Elen ad Ereivir

Special Thanks
Alban Barré
Stephan May